Reaching Skyward

James D. Hamilton Ed.D.

Copyright © 2017

REACHING SKYWARD

James D. Hamilton, Ed.D.

Dedication

To my friend of 71 years,
Kenneth Shelby Armstrong, Th.D., Ed.D.
pastor, educator, college vice-president,
college president, author, publisher,
of this book and many other publications.
His friendship is a gift to me for
which I am deeply grateful.

James D. Hamilton, Ed.D.

A Special Dedication

Affectionately dedicated to my parents

Mr. and Mrs. Jess Hamilton

Contents

PART THREE: The Outward Look   6

GOD'S THERENESS

Persons residing in the area of Colorado Springs, Colorado, have the privilege of living at the foot of the majestic mountain known as Pikes Peak. On a clear day, this massive product of God's creation can be seen for many miles. It is a landmark of marvelous beauty and mammoth proportions.

Sometimes atmospheric conditions are such that the peak is totally obscured from sight. Fog may fill the valleys, blocking it from view. But Pikes Peak is still there.

Blizzards may turn the sky into swirling white, making the mountain invisible, but it is still there. Every night the mountain is enveloped in darkness. It is out of sight, but it is still there.

Under these changing conditions, residents of that area do not ask, "Where is Pikes Peak? It was there only yesterday." They know it is there even though it cannot be seen. It need not be seen to be believed.

God is like that. His reality is not dependent upon visibility. The cynical sinner says that God is not real because he has never seen Him. This was so of the Russian cosmonaut who returned to earth and reported that he did not see God during his flight in space. Persons without faith are incapable of either seeing or finding God.

Saints can also fall into the error of equating God's reality with His visibility. Any one of a thousand things—discouragement, disillusionment, disease, defeat—may temporarily block one's view of God. But God is still there just the same. As Francis Schaeffer puts it, He is "the God who is there."

Faith enables us to be sure of the God we cannot see. It helps us to see the invisible. This is the meaning of Hebrews 11:1, which says, "Now faith is the substance of things hoped for, the evidence of things not seen."

Faith does not create God. It does not make something real out of that which is unreal. Rather, faith asserts the "thereness" of God, even in the absence of His visibility.

Faith never asks, "Where is God?" Rather, faith points with a steady finger and confidently declares, "*God is there.*"

May God help us to exercise a faith that affirms His "thereness"!

CHRIST THE KING

Jesus' accusers wanted to kill Him. But to do so they had to have the consent of Pilate. When Pilate called them for consultation, they would not enter his palace because that would "defile" them, so Pilate went out to them. How absurd legalism is! It is unwilling to yield at a minor point of the law, yet is quite willing to take an innocent life.

Pilate asked the Jewish leaders a direct question, "What is His crime?" Their response avoided the question: "We would not have arrested an innocent man, would we?" They responded indirectly because He had done no crime. They found fault *with* Him, but they could find no fault *in* Him. Neither could Pilate.

The accusers were incensed because Jesus called himself King of the Jews. "Are You?" Pilate asked. Jesus replied, "Yes, I am a King. I was born for this purpose, and My mission is to bring truth to the world" (cf. John 18:37). In one breath Jesus stated *what* He was and *why* He came a heavenly King whose purpose was to bring truth to an ignorant world.

His kingdom is like no other kingdom. Other kingdoms are based on power; Christ's kingdom is based on truth. Other kingdoms are measured in miles; the dimensions of Christ's kingdom are the dimensions of the human heart.

No king was ever like Christ the King. Other kings came to conquer and control; Christ came to lift and liberate. He holds no weapon save the sword of truth and He possesses only what is given to Him. He came to give, not to get; to build, not to destroy; to give life, not to take it.

Christ the King did not march to the strains of "Pomp and Circumstance"; rather, He quietly rode on a lowly donkey. He owned no regal robe and His only ornamentation was that of a meek and quiet spirit. But a King He was and no other has been His equal.

Earthly kings must fight to maintain their position (John 8:36) but Jesus' position was established by Almighty God and it needed no defense. Jesus *was* King. He *is* King. He will *always* be King.

PROPHECY FULFILLED IN CHRIST

How sad those two disciples were! Discouraged, disillusioned and disheartened, they walked wearily along the Emmaus road. Joined by the risen Christ, whom they did not recognize, they fell into conversation with Him. Telling of Jesus' death, they said, "But we trusted that it had been he which should have redeemed Israel" (Luke 24:21).

Had they really trusted that Christ was the Messiah? The answer is clearly no. Theirs had not been a trust in Christ; rather, it had been a desperate human hope. Because their hope had not been grounded in God's Word, it quickly degenerated into discouragement.

From the time of Moses some 1,500 years before, the prophets had foretold the coming of Christ. How easily should these two disciples have trusted Christ when He came! How quickly their hopes shattered when He died!

Trust is one of the grandest words in the Christian's vocabulary. It means to put full confidence in the character of Christ. Christ's character and God's Word stand behind what He says. What a difference it would make if we would truly trust. Here is the secret:

11

Simply trusting ev'ry day,
Trusting thro' a stormy way;
Even when my faith is small,
Trusting Jesus, that is all.
                -EDGAR PAGE STITES

Jesus is not only our best Hope; He is our only Hope. There is salvation in none other, the Bible says (Acts 4:12). If we do not trust Christ, there is no point in trusting anyone else or anything else. Had those two Emmaus-bound disciples really accepted that simple, yet profound, truth, spiritual depression would never have claimed them

.
Let us not make the same error. Let us truly trust Him. He is the Messiah, just as the Bible for centuries has declared Him to be.

In spite of how dismal it may appear for the cause of Christ at any given moment, He is still the Messiah and His kingdom will prevail. The prophecies of the Scriptures have been fulfilled in Christ, and we are the recipients of God's grace made manifest in Him. Let us pray with William H. Bathurst:

> *O for a faith that will not shrink,*
> *Tho' pressed by every foe,*
> *That will not tremble on the brink*
> *Of any earthly woe!*

GOOD NEWS FOR ALL MEN

In the spring of 1973, the world was stirred while watching telecasts of the returning Vietnam prisoners of war. It was a delight to see the glow on their faces and it was a joy to hear them express their gratitude to be home after many years of captivity and painful isolation. Seeing those men coming home and being reunited with their ecstatically happy families was a never-to-be-forgotten experience. They were liberated.

But the earth has known a greater liberation. It occurred when Christ gave His life on the middle cross to redeem mankind. His sacrifice on Calvary made it possible for all men, not just a few, to be set free.

Every Vietnam prisoner of war lived with the hope that one day he would be released. It was that hope which kept him alive. But the redemption that Christ brought was for those who had no hope. What a dreadful thought: imprisoned without hope. But Christ changed that.

This is the good news of the ages: A divine Liberator has come to release *all* men from the prison house of sin. Let us rejoice today that Christ has come to bring His deliverance to us.

The belief in a limited atonement—salvation for a few—is a reflection on the character of an all-loving, merciful Heavenly Father. It is also an insult to the Saviour who poured out His life for every last son of Adam's lost race. Christ died for all. The songwriter expressed the liberation theme beautifully in these lines:

> *Lord, I believe, were sinners more*
> *Than sands upon the ocean shore,*
> *Thou hast for all a ransom paid,*
> *For all a full atonement made.*

The meaning of the word *gospel* is good news. But if it is not god news for all, then it is bad news for some. That being so, it would deny the essential meaning of the gospel. Here are two inescapable truths in the Bible: (1) All have sinned and (2) Christ died for all. God's cure is as pervasive as man's disease. "Where sin abounded, grace did much more abound." (Rom. 5:20)

THE SAVIOUR REJECTED AND KILLED

Fulton Oursler tells the story of a European doctor who developed a miracle cure. Soon he became famous and was invited to speak about his cure to medical groups throughout the world. Many persons deluged him with requests to heal them or their loved ones. His fame brought him to the United States for a lecture. He went for a walk and was caught in a sudden rainstorm. Hurrying to the nearest house, he knocked and asked for shelter from the storm.

The woman who answered his knock rudely turned him away. The next morning she was shocked to see his picture in the newspaper announcing his visit to the city. This very woman had earlier written the doctor, addressing him at the hotel where he would be staying, begging him to treat their daughter for the dreaded disease for which he had the cure.

The one she needed most was on her doorstep only hours before, but she had refused him an entrance. Similarly, the Saviour knocks at the door of the human heart with the only cure for the disease of sin. All too often He is rejected and denied an entrance.

In one of the Apostle Paul's greatest sermons (Acts 13:16-41), he told the Jews that Christ was from them, that He came to them and that He died for them. But the Jews rejected Jesus. The door of salvation, first opened only to the Jews, was opened to the Gentiles. Salvation became available to all through Christ

.

Our opportunity to receive Christ is just as glorious as that of the Jews and our rejection of Him can be just as disastrous. Salvation rejected is not salvation; it is damnation. What Christ did for us means nothing to us if it is not worked in us.

> *There's a Saviour who stands at the door of your heart.*
> *He is longing to enter—why let Him depart?*
> *He has patiently called you so often before,*
> *But you must open the door."*
> -INA DULEY OGDON

THE EXALTED KING

King David prophesied that Christ would come, that He would die, that He would be resurrected and that He would ascend to heaven to be with God the Father. This was a prophecy by a king of *the* King. It was a case of earthly nobility recognizing heavenly nobility.

On the Day of Pentecost, Peter's grand sermon declared that King David's prophecy had been fulfilled, that Christ the King had risen indeed, and that He occupied an exalted position in the heavens at the right hand of God. (Acts 2).

The worst that the Jews had done to Christ—death by crucifixion—had been nullified by the power of God's resurrection. Instead of being entombed in the earth, Christ was enthroned in the heavens.

He is still there, occupying His exalted position and making intercession for us. From that position He will come to receive His redeemed who shall share in His exaltation.

No grander thought can come to the human mind than to realize that the Christian will share in Christ's eternal kingdom. "Joint-heirs with Christ" is God's promise to His people (Rom. 8:17). What a transition—from death to life, from darkness to light, from nothing to everything.

Carl Boberg in his much-loved hymn, "How Great Thou Art," wrote of this glorious reality in these words:

> *When Christ shall come with shout of*
> *acclamation*
> *And take me home, what joys shall fill my*
> *heart!*
> *Then I shall bow in humble adoration*
> *And there proclaim, my God, how great*
> *Thou art!**

And praise Him we will, for we will know that this shared exaltation will be the result of grace, and grace alone. Knowing that our salvation and exaltation are granted, not earned, we will, in Edward Peronnet's words,

> *Bring forth the royal diadem,*
> *And crown Him Lord of all.*

Lord of all, and lord with Him. That is almost more than the mind of man can comprehend. But it is true and we have the word of God himself on it. Let us live in daily honor of our exalted King, realizing that He promised, "I will come again and receive you unto myself; that where I am, there ye may be also." (John 14:3)

CHRIST IS RISEN

One would not expect to find a well person in a hospital, nor would one assume that he could find a youth living in a retirement home. Similarly, it would be foolish to look for a live person in a cemetery, in the "silent city of the dead."

But that is what the women were doing on the first Easter morning—looking for Christ in a cemetery. With striking simplicity, the angels said to the women, "Why seek ye the living among the dead? He is not here, but is risen." (Luke 24:5-6). They were looking for Christ in the wrong place!

Jesus' grand declaration that He would rise on the third day had fallen on deaf ears. Therefore the women had gone sorrowfully to do service to His dead body on that Easter morning. Presuming Him to be dead, it was logical that they would look for Him in the tomb in which He had been placed on Friday afternoon. But a tomb is a place for the dead, not the living. The living Christ no longer had need for a tomb.

Let it be said, to our shame, that we, like those women, sometimes act as if Christ is yet in the tomb. But He is alive and His Church is on the march. His triumph over death gives us assurance that we, too, need not fear the future. His victory is our victory. Charles Wesley sounded the Easter message in these words:

> *Lives again our glorious King. Alleluia!*
> *Where, O death, is now thy sting? Alleluia!*
> *Dying once, He all doth save. Alleluia!*
> *Where thy victory, O grave? Alleluia!*

Let us lift up our heads and look full in the face of the risen Christ who has conquered our greatest enemy. A depressed spirit is a denial of the triumph of our risen Lord. He is not in a hole in the ground; He is at home in heaven. He is not locked in the jaws of death; He is risen!

This is the glorious truth of Christianity: Christ's tomb is empty! Thank God for the empty tomb and for the Christ who "is risen again, who is even at the right hand of God, who also maketh intercession for us." (Rom. 8:34).

CHRIST IS VICTOR OVER DEATH

Adam left the human race a legacy of drastic proportions—sickness, sadness, suffering, and death. Little did he know the magnitude of the consequences that would follow his act of disobedience in the Garden of Eden.

Since Adam, man has lived with the awesome reality that death would finally claim him. Death, the destination of a journey of despair. What a dismal end for man! In contrast to this darkness of despair is the reality of the Resurrection. The Resurrection sheds a glorious light of hope in the tomb by becoming "the firstfruits of them that slept." Christ's resurrection assures us that our last enemy, death, is only a small, dark vestibule through which we pass into everlasting light and life.

A little girl who was terrified by tunnels came to see that her intense fear of them was unnecessary. Later, she said to her mother, "I like tunnels—they have light at both ends."

No one relishes the thought of dying. Saint and

sinner shrink from the encounter with "the grim reaper." What is the difference, then, between the saint and the sinner as each faces the reality of death—of his own non-being? While both of them fear the *process* of death, the Christian does not fear the *consequence* of death. That is the difference.

The sinner's death is a sunset without a sunrise. The saint's death is a sunset that prepares the way for an eternal sunrise. Light at both ends—the light of Christ's grace today and the light of His resurrection tomorrow—is what God gives to the Christian. These two great lights are separated only by the short tunnel we call death. No wonder the Apostle Paul asked "O death, where is thy sting? O grave, where is thy victory?"

LIFE FOR DEATH

Unredeemed man is earthbound. He is *in* the world; he is *of* the world; and he is controlled *by* the world. He is born of the dust, lives in the dust, and will return to the dust. How helpless and hopeless he is!

Edna St. Vincent Millay, in her poem "Ashes of Life," describes the plight of men in the following lines:

> *Life goes on forever, like the gnawing of a*
> *mouse,*
> *And tomorrow, and tomorrow, and tomorrow*
> *There's this little street and this little house.*

These lines reflect the routine of meaninglessness which is characteristic of contemporary man. Worse yet is man's fate as he contemplates his future. Bryon Kent expresses this hopelessness as follows:

> *My life, like a vapour, shall soon be gone,*
> *But who on this earth shall my passing*
> *mourn?*

*How right was the man when he spoke "No
man careth for my soul."*

*The future holds but despair and gloom,
And time anxiously waits to seal my doom.
Only endless torture waits for me
In the black expanse of eternity.*

Thank God, that need not be the final picture of man. God has sent His Son into the world that man might live through Him. The life that He gives is spiritual life which brings meaning and purpose into man's earthbound existence. Christ brings an out-of-this-world dimension to man and enables him to live a life that is not of this world. He gives a bright future to a man with a black past and a drab present.

This is why Christ came to our world—to bring us abundant life from His world. As He said, "I am come that they might have life, and that they might have it more abundantly" (John 10:10). Life for death—only Christ can offer such an option to man.

JESUS IS LORD

The lordship of Christ is fully established by the Scriptures. No grander declaration of His lordship can be found than in Phil. 2:10-11, which says that "at the name of Jesus every knee should bow, of things in heaven, and things in earth, and things under the earth; and that every tongue should confess that Jesus is Lord, to the glory of God the Father."

Jesus deliberately laid His lordship aside in heaven in order to become a man on earth. Never was He farther from His lordship than when He died like a criminal on the Cross. What condescension, to leave the heights of heaven and descend to a death like that! The Bible says, "Even the death of the cross." (Phil. 2:8). Christ's death was the worst death possible—ignominious Roman crucifixion.

But God's purpose was working in it. Because of who Christ was (God's son) and what He is (man's Saviour), God exalted Him to heaven's highest honor. God's declaration was that Christ's name is above every name and at the name of Jesus *every* knee shall bow, both in heaven and in earth and *every* tongue shall confess that Jesus Christ is Lord.

There is a difference between the universal lordship and the particular lordship of Christ. While it is objectively true that Christ is Lord in the universal sense, that truth has meaning only in the subjective, personal sense. While Christ is potentially Lord to everyone, He is Lord to no one except as He is Lord to each one. Angelus Silesius expressed this truth in these lines:

> *Though Christ a thousand times*
> *In Bethlehem be born,*
> *If He's not born in thee*
> *Thy soul is still forlorn.*
> *The cross on Golgotha*
> *Will never save thy soul,*
> *The cross in thine own heart*
> *Alone can make thee whole.*

Personal, not universal, salvation is the only salvation that matters. There is no Redeemer until He is *my* Redeemer and *my* lord.

THE KING IS COMING

The prophet Zechariah promised that God's people would have a king: "Rejoice greatly, O daughter of Zion; shout, O daughter of Jerusalem: behold, thy King cometh unto thee: he is just, and having salvation; lowly, and riding upon an ass, and upon a colt the foal of an ass." (9:9).

What hope this promise brought! To a defeated, discouraged, disheartened people would come a King. He did not come grandly as they thought He would come; He came meekly as the Scriptures said He would come. He did not come in a war chariot, symbolizing power; He came riding a donkey, symbolizing humanity and peace.

Christ the King did not come to conquer the world. He did not have to conquer what was already His. It was Christ who brought both earth and heaven into existence (John 1:3). The Psalmist announced, "The heavens declare the glory of God; and the firmament sheweth his handiwork." (19:1).

Christ stands over His creation and He is in control of it. He is the Owner of all and Lord of all. In the light of who He is and what He has done, mankind joins with all of nature in declaring that Christ is King indeed. "Who is the King of glory? The Lord of hosts, he is the King of glory." (Ps. 24:10).

If Christ did not come to conquer the earth, why did He come? He came to conquer sin, and He did it in one mighty saving act on Cavalry. When He uttered the words "It is finished" from the Cross, He declared that Satan's power would ultimately be destroyed because of His complete sacrifice for sin.

Let all Christians rejoice. The King came once and He is coming again. His first coming was to conquer sin; His second coming will be to gather His redeemed.

The Apostle Paul referred to Christ's second coming as "that blessed hope" (Titus 2:13). A blessed hope it is. His coming will mark the end of sorrow and struggle, and all Christians will be released to joy and peace as we reign with Christ in His glorious kingdom.

Yes, the King is coming. "Rejoice . . . shout . . . thy King cometh unto thee" (Zech. 9:9).

WHAT'S IN A NEST?

F. W. Boreham said that a cuckoo sometimes lays her eggs in a robin's nest. These strangers in the nest hatch out alongside the baby robins.

At first the parents are mystified at the presence of foreigners among their brood. In time the growing cuckoos push the baby robins out of the nest to die on the ground. Nevertheless, the parent robins continue to feed the murderers of their own offspring, treating them as their own.

This is not a phenomenon confined to the world of birds. It also happens in human experience as related to sin. Satan has a subtle way of slipping sin into one's life. If sin is not disposed of "before it hatches," it has a way of growing and taking over. Alexander Pope expressed this truth in the following lines:

Vice is a monster of so frightful mien,
As to be hated needs but to be seen;
But seen too oft, familiar with her face,
We first endure, then pity, then embrace.

Note the sequence: endure, pity, embrace. Once sin is allowed to become commonplace and familiar, one is on the road to embracing it for his own.

Not a few persons are embracing sins which they once abhorred. The reasons for doing so are many, but not the least among them is that the egg was not thrown from the nest at the moment it was laid. Time made it a member of the family.

The Scriptures are clear at the point of one's attitude toward sin. The instruction is to deal with it instantly. The Apostle Paul enjoined Christians to shun the very "appearance of evil." (1 Thess. 5:22). By doing so, sin will not be permitted to hatch out and take over the life.

In some segments of the Christian Church a relaxed and friendly attitude is being taken toward sins which once were considered abhorrent. If we do not remain spiritually perceptive, we could fall into the same error, causing us to condone the sins which we are called to condemn. Let us check the nest and throw out the foreign eggs before they hatch and do their deadly work.

SILENT SINS

Clyde Beatty, who trained lions and tigers for years and was mauled over 100 times, died of cancer. There is a spiritual lesson in that. Our greatest dangers are not those that are without. On the contrary, we run the greatest risk of spiritual death from the silent sins on the inside.

These silent sins may not seem as threatening as the snarling sins on the outside, but they are deadly nonetheless. Because they are silent, internal, and out of sight, they pose our greatest threat.

An unforgiving spirit is one of the silent sins that can destroy spiritual life. One can have an unforgiving spirit, and it may never be known by others. Worse yet, one may have such a spirit and scarcely be aware of himself.

But it takes a toll—silently, slowly, and surely eating away the person from the inside. Jesus taught us that if we do not forgive those who have wronged us, neither will the Father forgive us.

Greed is another silent sin. It attacks from the inside, making it difficult to detect. Sometimes greed goes under the guise of a search for security, causing one to center his interests on material things rather than things of the spirit.

Peter Marshall called materialism "the hook that is baited with security." Jesus knew the great dangers of materialism and had more to say about it than He did about heaven.

A wrong motive is another silent sin that can destroy a person from the inside. A wrong motive is sometimes difficult to detect because it can express itself in good behavior. But if the right action is performed for the wrong reason, its virtue is nullified. God, who "looketh on the heart," sees a person as he really is, and judges the motive for the behavior, not the act itself.

Resentment is another silent sin that takes its toll of the spirit. To resent is to re-feel a hurt. One who resents assumes that he is repaying his offender. What he fails to realize is that the resentment affects the resenter more than it affects the resented.

Beware of the silent sins which are capable of destroying from the inside.

MAN-EATERS

Major Jim Corbett was a professional hunter hired by the government of India to kill man-eating tigers. In his book *Man-eaters of Kumaon*, he stated that often tigers become man-eaters because of old wounds that never heal.

Once Corbett was called to an Indian village to kill a tiger that had been terrorizing the natives. One night, as he lay in wait, the tiger slinked through the village, making a low, moaning, groaning sound as he walked. When morning came, Corbett tracked and killed the huge animal. When it was skinned, he found that an old wound near the base of a leg had festered and putrified. That was the reason for the moans of pain it had made as it walked through the village. That was also the reason why it had become a man-eater. No longer able to compete in the animal world for its food, it turned on helpless humans.

Old wounds can turn people into man-eaters, too. A hurt, either real or imagined, can fester and putrify, causing one to turn on others for revenge. The man-eating spirit causes the death of relationships. It divides homes, splits churches and brings pain to many. The greatest pain, however, is experienced by the one who carries the un-healed wound. Like the tiger, with each step the agonizing pain of the old wound is felt. It is dual pain: the original hurt, plus the pain of its infection.

In life's relationships, particularly the intimate ones, we are susceptible to hurts. Persons who love deeply can also suffer deeply. The question is not *if* we will be hurt in life. We will. The issue is what we permit our hurts to do *in* us. What happens *to* us and what happens *in* us are two very different matters.

There are two ways of dealing with our hurts: (1) Let the wounds fester, or (2) Permit the cleansing power of the Holy Spirit to bring healing to the wounded spirit. The first way is man's reaction *to* hurt; the second way is God's solution *for* hurt. God's way is the best way.

THE TIMELESS QUALITY OF GUILT

She has everything a woman could want except a happy marriage. She is young, attractive, intelligent, educated, creative and energetic. Her children are bright and healthy. Her husband is successful and wealthy. She has a large, beautiful home in the country, her own sports car, several horses, a trail bike, and all the money she needs. But she is unhappy because she is not fulfilled in her marriage.

This unhappiness was her excuse for seeking the companionship of another man. This culminated in an illicit sexual relationship. Torn by guilt, she sought the help of a Christian counselor. She told him of her guilt and how she tried to find relief by engaging in her hobby of oil painting. She stated, "But when I clean out my brushes, there's life again." By this she meant that her knowledge of guilt returned.

Hers is an age-old attempt to handle guilt by diverting the mind to other matters in the hope that it will go away. Guilt cannot be disposed of that easily. It has a way of coming back after the brushes are cleaned out. Of course, it is there all the time, but temporarily submerged through diversion.

Some believe that guilt will lose its power with the passing of time. But guilt has a timeless quality. Each year the Internal Revenue Service receives money from the guilt-ridden persons who pay back taxes. In some cases the cheating was done years earlier, but the guilt persisted until the payment was made.

The timeless quality of guilt is clearly illustrated in the biblical story of the brothers of Joseph who sold him into slavery. In spite of the passing of time—possibly as much as 20 years—they confessed, "We are verily guilty concerning our brother." (Gen. 42:21). They did not say that they *were* guilty. The act which produced guilt was in the past tense but their guilt was in the present tense. "We are guilty," they said. Their guilt was present, painfully present. Guilt is always in the present tense.

Man is not capable of handling his guilt. That is why Christ came—to provide a means of resolving sin and guilt through His atoning blood. Through confession, repentance and faith in Christ, the sin is forgiven and the guilt is removed. That is God's way to handle guilt and it is the only way.

BEHIND THE MASK

Thomas Babington Macauley said, "The measure of a man's real character is what he would do if he knew he would never be found out." How true that is.

Behind the mask of how a man appears is the man as he really is. The man "out front" may be the epitome of kindness, gentleness, truth and honesty; the man behind may be quite different. The real person is the person who is behind and out of sight.

The Watergate scandals of the seventies illustrate this perfectly. Men who seemed to be of stature and character were found to be the opposite. Behind the masks of integrity and goodness were the real men of dishonesty and badness. The men who stooped to such crime never dreamed they would be found out.

The men who were tried and sentenced were not the men "out front." Had this been so, not one would have been guilty. No, the men behind the masks—the men as they really were—were the guilty ones.

There is a risk in living behind a facade. However, carefully one covers his deceit, there is always the danger of being found out. Even if one is not discovered in his duplicity, he carries with him the knowledge of his evil deeds. One can become his own prisoner even though his crime is not discovered. Epictetus said, "No bad man is truly free." There is a great wisdom in that statement.

The mask a person wears is an attempt to conceal from others what one truly is. Sometimes the deception is successful; sometimes it is not. But God is never fooled. While man looks at the outward appearance, God looks at the heart (1 Sam. 16:7). God ignores man's reputation and sees his character. He looks through the mask and sees this man. "The heart is . . . desperately wicked: who can know it?" (Jer. 17:9). The answer is: man, sometimes; God, always.

HABITS

A curious sight is a cucumber in a bottle which is larger than the bottle's neck. The question is "How did it get there?" The answer is that the bottle was slipped over the cucumber when it was small, and it grew to full size within the bottle.

Habits are like that. They start as a tiny growth within a person and grow until they reach the size that they cannot be removed. Someone has said, "The chains of habit are too weak to be felt until they are too strong to be broken." That is the nature of habits—they *seem* harmless but, given some time to develop, they become larger than a person's power to remove.

The alcoholic begins his miserable existence by taking "a small, harmless drink." Multiplied many times over, the small, harmless drink becomes a monster which has him under its control. He would readily pay anything he has for one more drink. Sometimes the price for a drink is the loss of a family or a future. But pay it he will, for he has no choice. He does not have a habit; the habit has him.

It is easy to see what the power of habit does to the alcoholic. Before we cast a stone, however, we should examine the power of habit in our own lives. Without scarcely knowing it, we can develop habits that control us. While not as obvious as alcoholism, we can engage in behaviors and attitudes which adversely affect our Christian witness.

One such habit is that of a critical attitude. People see what they look for. Della Crowder Miller wrote:

> *Two walked in my garden*
> *Through soft, sunny hours;*
> *The one saw but weeds,*
> *The other saw flowers.*

The critical habit resists change. An old gentleman was being interviewed on his one-hundreth birthday. The interviewer said, "I suppose you have seen a lot of changes in your lifetime." The man replied, "Yes, and I have been against every one of them." Such an attitude has slowed the progress of countless churches.

Let us look for the habits that hinder us from becoming what God has intended us to be and pray that His grace will remove them from us.

HURLING HALOS

The police department does not classify a halo as a lethal weapon. Nobody does. In fact, it is usually viewed as the opposite of an implement of evil. Nevertheless, it can be used as a deadly weapon. Just how does one hurl a halo?

Hurling a halo is the art of using a judgmental attitude under the guise of deep spirituality. It is using one's strengths to reveal another's weaknesses. It is designed to make oneself look good while making others look bad.

A most effective time to hurl a halo is during public prayer. Under these sanctimonious auspices one can pray in such a way as to hit a target up to 40 paces (a distance greater than the length of most sanctuaries).

This is done by praying in such a manner as to all but name "those of our number who are not faithful to all of our services," or "those who are not standing by the work of God with their tithes and offerings," or "those who have not been attending the sunrise prayer meeting."

The ideal position for hurling such a halo is from

the platform of the sanctuary. The slight downward direction from this elevated position makes the heave more effective.

The halo can become effective when hurled at ranges greater than the dimensions of the local church. Halos have been known to be hurled all the way to the district center: "The heavy budgets that keep our little church from meeting its own needs."

Sometimes a halo can be hurled across an entire educational zone: "We can't conscientiously give sanctified money to a church college that permits students to wear their hair *that* long."

Who knows but with a little practice you many acquire the skill of hurling your halo all the way to Kansas City. Some have.

There is a risk in hurling the halo. One must be careful not to be guilty of what he condemns in others. In such a case the halo becomes a boomerang and the result can be embarrassing—as embarrassing as trying to pick a splinter out of another's eye when one has a log in his own.

ON CHOOSING

Four-year old David was faced with the pleasant task of choosing between two attractive alternatives: (1) going to the airport to watch a houseguest depart on a huge jet, or (2) staying home and watching "Sesame Street" on television. With a child's genius for insight he said, "My heart can't make up its mind what to do."

Wouldn't it be great if all of our choices were such that either option could be good, that either could bring us legitimate pleasure?

In the little boy's case there was no possibility of a wrong choice. The excitement of the air terminal, with the hope of a candy bar from a vending machine as an added bonus, was most attractive. On the other hand, watching "Sesame Street", along with full refrigerator privileges, offered a delight one could not easily decline. No wonder his heart could not make up its mind what to do!

Unfortunately, the opportunity of choosing between two equally good options occurs rarely. Rather, choices are usually between a good and a lesser good, or between good and bad. In such cases it is imperative that the right choice be made, because each choice carries its own consequences. To say it another way, we have the power to choose but we do not have the power to change the consequences of our choices. So it is essential that we carefully weigh our choices.

How awesome is the power of choice! God can aid us in our choices but He does not make our choices for us. Moses, speaking for God, said to the Israelites, "I have set before you life and death, blessing and cursing: therefore choose life." (Deut. 30:19).

Neither does God alter the consequences of our choices. Of the same Israelites it was said that God "gave them their request; but sent leanness into their soul." (Ps. 106:15). God did not stop the Israelites in their wrong choice, nor did He stop the resulting outcome—leanness of soul. Leanness of soul was the inevitable consequence of opting for less than God's best.

When the heart "can't make up its mind what to do," let us remember to choose for God and for good.

TRUST

Trust is the strongest word describing the Christian's relationship with God. It is defined in the following ways: "assured reliance on God's integrity," "to place full confidence in God," "a reliance on God based upon experience and association." Trust is something man *does* based on what he believes God *is*; it centers in the very character of God himself.

Trust is illustrated by the story of a scientist who wanted to hire a little boy to retrieve some rare bird eggs from a nest on the side of a steep cliff. The operation required that the boy be lowered by rope over the cliff. The boy agreed on the following condition: "Only if my father holds the rope." There you have it. Trust is simple if the right Person is at the other end of the rope.

Proverbs 3 gives clear instructions regarding trust. The Lord is to be trusted with all the heart (v. 5). That means that one's very being is to be placed in God's care. With confidence in God, man is to stake his very life upon Him. Man is warned not to lean on his own understanding (v. 5). That means that self-trust is to be distrusted.

Trusting is acting based on believing. Remember, however, that the belief must be in God, not self.

Much of the current "self-help religion" is based on belief. But the belief is in man's ability to transcend himself. Thus the focus is on man, not God. That is why it often becomes an exercise in futility. Bishop William Quale, pressed with many difficulties, said that one night he found himself restless and sleepless as he fretted over his problems. He reported that the Lord said, "Now, William, you go to sleep and I'll sit up." How easy it is to cease trusting God and begin trusting self. But this transfer of trust always results in frustration.

When one has truly trusted in God, only then can he trust himself: "In all thy ways acknowledge him, and he shall direct thy paths." (Prov. 3:6). One cannot be both navigator and pilot of his own life, but if God is the Navigator, it is no problem to be the pilot.

GOD'S RICH PAUPERS

God made a threefold promise to Abraham: (1) that his descendents would be many; (2) that his people would be given a land as their inheritance; and (3) that from his people would come a Redeemer. These promises sustained Israel through many periods of problems and persecutions.

Following their exodus from Egypt and their wanderings in the wilderness, God gave the Israelites a glorious conquest of Canaan. They were back in their own land! Prophecy had been fulfilled; God had kept His promise.

After the conquest, the tribes met to allocate the land. What an exciting time it must have been to see the fulfillment of God's promise! Added to the thrill for the whole nation was the more immediate excitement running through each tribe: Where will we be located? How good will our land be? Will we be able to get rich quick?

The land was divided and each tribe received its allotment. There were 12 tribes but only 11 received land. The Levites were left out because they were the priestly tribe, and God had decreed that they should not receive land. Poor Levites— no land, no security. They must have felt like the nephew at the reading of his rich uncle's will. The lawyer read, ". . . and to my nephew, who always wanted to be remembered in my will—'Hello, Charlie.'"

Land then, as now, represented value, but the Levites were given none. That is not all of the story. The Bible says, "The Lord God of Israel was their inheritance" (Josh. 13:33). What a thought— they inherited God! That is the ultimate in riches. The Levites were God's rich paupers. In getting God, they got everything.

Material wealth never brings lasting satisfaction; it brings only the desire for more. When asked how much it takes to satisfy a person, Rockefeller said, "Just a little bit more."

But God is the satisfying Portion, and the Levites received Him. In inheriting God, they received more than any tribe and more than all of the tribes added together.

Through Christ all of us can inherit God. He said that He came to give us the abundant life (John 10:10). This is the life that is in God. And when we receive Him, we receive all that He *is* plus all that He *has*. Like the Levites, ours is wealth untold. What a great inheritance!

SAINT UNDER CONSTRUCTION

A defendant in a hard-fought civil case who had pleaded "Not guilty" changed his plea to "Guilty" toward the end of his trial.

He explained to the surprised judge, "I thought I was innocent, but at that time I had not heard all the evidence against me."

This humorous incident points out the tendency in human nature to be blind to one's faults.

Reality to any person is how he perceives it. If one cannot see his faults, he assumes he is innocent. But like the defendant, this "innocence" can be challenged by external, verifiable data. When the evidence is in, the plea must be changed to "Guilty."

God's Word has the capacity to clearly reveal man as he is. It shows one that he is not as he perceives himself to be. That is why one must continuously expose himself to the searching truth of the Bible. If we follow the tendency of human nature, we will become blind to our faults and our needs. If we expose ourselves to the Word, it is like seeing ourselves in a high-quality, well-polished mirror, revealing us as we really are.

It is not God's purpose merely to prove us wrong. Rather, He seeks to make us right after we have seen our wrong.

God has no finished saints on earth. On each of His children hangs a sign which says, "Saint Under Construction."

Converts are made in an instant, but it takes longer to make a saint. This is because making a saint is a joint effort between God and the Christian. On the part of the person it takes openness to one's need and the willingness to improve. On the part of God it takes communication through His Word and leading by His Spirit.

It is a mistake to assume that Christian maturity is attained automatically with the passing of time. It is achieved by an earnest desire to see ourselves as we are and a determination to become what God wants us to be. That takes time and much effort. It also takes grace, much grace.

Let us expose ourselves to God's Word, so that we may see ourselves as He sees us, in order that we may become what He wants us to become.

BUILDING FOR ETERNITY

Somebody's dream was shattered. The dream was a leisure home built high in the Colorado Rockies. But it was never enjoyed, because it was destroyed by extremely heavy snows which collapsed the roof and separated the walls. It lay in shambles. All of the money, labor, and time invested in it was lost. It did not survive the first winter.

The builder made two related mistakes: (1) He did not reckon with the possibility that the coming winter could bring the heaviest snowfall the area had had in years; and (2) He did not provide enough bracing in the roof to withstand the enormous weight of the snow. As a result, the home was destroyed.

It is sad when anyone's dream is shattered. Most tragic it is when the loss is spiritual. Not a few persons have had high hopes for their lives but never succeeded in reaching their goals. Like the builder, they did not realize the enormous pressure that life could bring, nor did they build into their lives the inner braces that would be needed to withstand great stress. As a result, their lives collapsed and their dreams were shattered.

One of God's great purposes is to give us the inner strength to withstand the worst that life can bring to us. He seeks to help us in the building of our lives so that we can stand when others fall. Someone has said that time will tell whether a man lays a good foundation for his life. That is true. But upon a solid foundation one must build each aspect of his life, so that it can survive pressure from all directions.

The building of a sturdy life takes planning, time and effort on the part of the Christian and much grace from God. Building a strong life is always a joint effort. We cannot build our lives without God's help. He will not build them without ours. John Wesley said of the early Methodists that they died well. This was so because they lived well. And they both lived well and died well because they built well.

We are building for eternity. Let us seek the aid of the eternal God who alone can help us build lives that will still be standing when others have fallen.

SAVED BY A CROSS

On February 7, 1958, United Press reported that a Los Angeles youth was shot in the chest during an attempted robbery. The slug was stopped by an inch-long cross that hung around his neck. Officers said that the four arms of the cross curled tightly around the slug and kept it from killing the youth. How symbolic that is—a sinner saved by a cross!

Such an incident of literally being saved by a cross may never have happened in history before. Yet what it symbolizes has occurred multiplied millions of times since Calvary. Every person who has claimed Christ as Lord has been saved by a cross.

The Cross was provided for man while he was in his sinful state—in the very act of sinning. The Apostle Paul said that "while we were yet sinners, Christ died for us." (Rom. 5:8). The fact that Christ died for us while we were sinners points up graphically that salvation is not granted on the basis of merit. Our very unworthiness combined with our helplessness caused Christ to climb to Calvary.

In the case of the young man whose life was saved by the cross, it was his only defense against death. Even so, the cross of Christ is our only defense against eternal death (Acts 4:12).

The knowledge that we have been saved by the Cross should cause us to respond in the following ways:

1. We should continuously express our thanks to Christ for His love to us. When memory drives us to the Cross, gratitude should drive us to our knees.
2. We should gladly share the news of Christ's salvation with others. That which is worth having is worth sharing.
3. We should make certain that our hope of heaven centers in God's grace, not in our own works. At the last day when we stand before God, may we be able to say:

> *Nothing in my hand I bring;*
> *Simply to Thy cross I cling.*
> —AUGUSTUS TOPLADY

LIFE-BUILDING

An Indian was carving a canoe out of a huge log. A friend said, "Chief, I think she's too wide for her length." So the Indian narrowed it down. Later, another man told him the stern was too wide, so he cut it down. A third person suggested that the bow needed changing, so he changed it.

When the canoe launched, it capsized. He hauled it to the beach, found another log, and began again. Once more a man came along and offered advice. Pointing to the previously completed monstrosity, the Indian said, "That boat over there is everybody's boat. This boat is *my* boat."

Many persons will attempt to tell us how to build our lives. But there is danger in designing our lives according to the directions of others. In so doing, we run the risk of capsizing and, unlike the Indian, we do not get the opportunity of a second try.

To be sure, we need help in building our lives; so God has given us two kinds of directions which we can follow. One is an outer set of directions and the other is inner. The outer set is God's Word; the inner set is the guidance of the Holy Spirit.

These two sets of directions never contradict each other. They are mutually supportive. If we pay close attention to the Holy Bible and the Holy Spirit, we can be assured of building the kind of life that will stand the test of time.

The Bible tells us that we are to make certain additions to our faith: virtue, knowledge, temperance, patience, godliness, brotherly kindness, and charity. By so doing we shall never fall (nor sink!) (2 Pet. 1:5-10).

If others give us directions for living that are supported by the Word and the Spirit, let us thank them for the reminder. On the other hand, if their directions cannot be so verified, let us ignore them and go on about our task of life-building.

What if Noah had accepted ark-building directions from his contemporaries? Human history would have ended with the Flood. Instead, Noah carefully followed God's blueprints and "prepared an ark to the saving of his house." (Heb. 11:7).

May God help us to do the same thing.

LET THE LORD HAVE THAT

Rev. Martin Luther King, Sr., experienced a triple tragedy between 1968 and 1974: the assassination of one son, the drowning of another, and the murder of his wife. Through it all, he did not question God, nor did he "charge God foolishly." (Job 1:22). Following the death of his wife, he said, "I know that God is not going to willfully hurt us. *Why* there is suffering is the business of the Lord, but He never seems to give us any more than we can bear."

The unwillingness to question the character of God is a mark of a committed Christian. When tragedy strikes a sinner, he questions God's character. When tragedy strikes the Christian, he may ask, "Why?" but he does not question the integrity of God. A Welsh Sunday school teacher instructed his class of boys, "Whatever ye do, lads, keep the character of God clear."

Therein lies the secret of the committed life: keeping the character of God clear. The kind of God some people have is a God not worth loving or serving. Indescribably evil acts are sometimes attributed to God, such as causing wars, killing babies, sending diseases, and a number of other things which are an insult to an all-loving Providence.

An angered parishioner once asked her pastor, "Would it surprise you if I told you I hated God?" He replied, "No, and if I had the kind of God you have, I would hate Him, too." The pastor knew that she was living with a distorted image of the nature and character of God. His response was not an assessment of God as He is; rather, it was an assessment of God as perceived by his parishioner.

When his wife was killed, Rev. King asserted, "I am not going to question the ways of the Lord or ask myself why this came about. His reasons will be known. But this I can assure you. I am not going to hate."

How could a person who experienced enough grief to make most persons deeply bitter bear the sorrow which came to him? In an interview following the senseless and tragic murder of his wife, he gave the answer to that question. He said that during his childhood days in rural Georgia, he often heard his saintly mother say, "Let the Lord have that." That is the secret: letting the Lord have what we cannot understand.

"Letting the Lord have that" is the life of commitment. It is a deliberate, willful act of surrendering to God what comes to us. Such commitment lets God be God without questioning

His character. It is keeping the character of God clear.

The committed life is letting God handle what we cannot handle. It is letting Him bear what we cannot bear. It is understanding that He understands what we cannot understand.

When suffering comes, let the Lord have that. He can handle it. If you try to handle it, you will experience the frustration of trying to understand a mystery, the solution of which has eluded the mind of man throughout the ages.

When sorrow comes, let the Lord have that. Be assured that God's promise is that Christ can give "beauty for ashes, the oil of joy for mourning, and the garment of praise for spirit of heaviness" (Isa. 61:3). The Psalmist said that the Lord heals the broken in heart and binds up their wounds (Ps. 147:3).

When disappointment comes, let the Lord have that. God knows how you feel, and He can help you with your feelings. His grace will be sufficient for you. When life hands you its worst, hand it back to God. "Let the Lord have that": this is the secret of consecrated living.

THE LISTENING SILENCE

Before the days of refrigeration, icehouses were used for cooling purposes. They had thick walls, no windows, and a tightly fitted door. In winter, when the streams and lakes were frozen, large blocks of ice were cut and stored in the icehouses and covered with sawdust. Often the ice would last well into the summer.

On one occasion a workman lost a valuable watch while working in an icehouse. He searched diligently for it, carefully raking through the sawdust, but his search was in vain. His fellow workers also tried to help him, but their efforts, too, proved futile. A small boy, who witnessed the fruitless search, slipped into the icehouse during the noon hour and soon emerged with the watch. Amazed at his success, the men asked him how he did it. He replied, "I closed the door, lay down in the sawdust, and kept very still. Soon I heard the watch ticking."

What a lesson there is in that. The Bible says that God speaks to us in a still, small voice. If we are still and listen for his His voice, He will guide us to himself.

The treasures of God are found in the quiet time. In moments of solitude and meditation we can be drawn to Him by the still, small voice. We do not find Him through our own anxious efforts; rather, we are drawn to Him through the quiet, listening silence. God's voice cannot be heard in the din of traffic that characterizes contemporary life. He is not found through our furious, frantic striving. Rather, as we close the door to the world outside, lay prostrate before Him, quiet out hearts in His presence, and listen for His voice, we will find Him.

Jesus told us that when we pray, we are to enter our closet, shut the door, and then pray to our Father who is in secret. If we do so, He said that the Father would reward us openly. (Matt. 6:6). And what a reward it is! As Augustine said, "The reward of God is himself."

It is the listening silence which brings us into the presence of the Lord. His instruction is, "Be still, and know that I am God." (Ps. 46:10).

PRAYER AND PRAISE

Earth's sorrows cause God's people to pray more often than they praise. While there is much for which we should praise God, the struggles of living in a sin-stained society cause us to lose sight of those things for which we should praise Him. In the midst of sickness and suffering, it seems that prayer is a more natural response than praise.

But this will not always be so. The promise is that God shall wipe away all the tears from our eyes; and there shall be no more death, sorrow, crying, or pain. (Rev. 21:4). What a day for praise that will be! It will be the first day since the Fall in the Garden of Eden that all of man's enemies will be eternally eliminated.

If heaven were only the absence of tears, death, sorrow, crying, and pain, it would be heaven enough. But heaven will be greater still because we will be reunited with loved ones. Besides that we will be united with the saints of all ages in the eternal presence of the Christ who bought our salvation with the price of His own blood. "Worthy is the Lamb that was slain" will be the song of the saved as we give glory to the Saviour who gave us victory over the worst that Satan could do to us. More than conquerors, we will be kings and priests with Christ forever and forever. These familiar words express it best:

> *When we've been there ten thousand years,*
> *Bright, shining as the sun,*
> *We've no less days to sing God's praise*
> *Than when we first begun.*
> —JOHN NEWTON

Until that day comes, let us remember to both pray and praise, remembering that we need to do both. Prayer can give birth to praise even in life's darkest hour. Did not Isaiah say that Jesus would give beauty for ashes, the oil of joy for mourning, and the garment of praise for the spirit of heaviness? (61:3)

TWO KINDS OF PRAISE

John 12 contains the record of two kinds of praise given to Jesus. The first was the praise of action performed by Mary when she anointed the feet of Jesus with very costly perfume. The second kind was verbal praise offered by the crowd which placed palm branches on the road to Jerusalem while crying, "Hosanna." as Jesus passed by.

Mary's praise was without fanfare. It was done in silent tribute to the Christ who had done so much for her. The crowd's praise was for show, and it was given for what they felt He *would* do rather than for what He *had* done. Mary's was the kind of praise that expected no response; the crowd's was praise with "strings attached."

Sacred history shows that the crowd's praise was insincere, and it turned to hatred in a matter of a few days. Mary's praise of love was with deep sincerity. Jesus said that her act would be a living memorial of selfless giving.

Jesus stated that it is possible for persons to praise Him with their lips while their hearts are far from Him. (Matt. 15:8). He knows that the words of men do not necessarily reflect their attitudes. But praise that takes the form of silent action involves one's inner person, his very self. It is done without display and without thought of a return reward.

There is a distinct difference between praise and flattery. On the surface they appear and sound the same. The way that praise and flattery can be distinguished is to examine the underlying motive of each. Praise is honor bestowed on another because he is worthy of praise either for his conduct or for his character. Flattery, on the other hand, is built upon a false base. It is not offered in sincerity. It is granted for the benefit of the bestower, not the bestowed. As such, it is counterfeit and of no value regardless of how authentic it appears.

Sincere verbal praise to Christ is appropriate. But a higher form of praise is that of loving action. Let praise to Christ be given in both word and deed.

SHOOTING STRAIGHT

The *Indiana Bell News* reported that an FBI marksman passed through a small town and saw evidence of amazing shooting accuracy. Painted on trees, walls, fences and buildings were numerous bull's-eyes with bullet holes in the exact center of each. He searched and found that the marksman was the village idiot. Asked how he could shoot so accurately, he replied, "I shoot first and draw the circle afterwards."

Some persons approach the matter of personal ethics in the same manner. They act first and evaluate their action later. Instead of using an external, objective norm for their behavior and prejudging actions in the light of it, they place their own value judgments on past performance. This is a delightfully easy method of managing personal ethics. However, the problem is that it is built upon the fallacy that man has the capacity for determining right and wrong. If one adheres to that philosophy, it is surprising how little he does that is wrong and how much he does that is right.

Drawing the bull's-eye around the hole—adjusting ethics to behavior—is the direct opposite of God's requirement for right living. He sets the standard and requires man to adjust to it. He never adjusts His standards to the performance of the person. Were He to do so, right and wrong would soon lose their meaning, and human behavior would lose its objective, ethical base.

Assessing behavior on the basis of human norms is not a new phenomenon. The surge of situation ethics in the sixties suggested that man had found a novel approval to personal ethics. Not so. One of the darkest, most chaotic ages in human history was during the period of the Judges. Sin was both flagrant and abundant. The Bible tells us why this was so: "Every man did that which was right in his own eyes." (Judg. 17:6). "Situation ethics" is as old as mankind.

The Psalmist said of the Israelites, "Like a crooked arrow, they missed the target of God's will." (Ps. 78:57, TLB). Crooked arrows can never hit God's target. Adjusting the target to crooked behavior never satisfies the demands of Diety. Straight shooting into the center of God's will is the only bull's-eye of behavior that counts.

CONTRIBUTION OR COMMITMENT?

A modern fable tells of a hen and a hog who were travelling together. They passed a church that displayed the sermon subject for the coming Sunday. It read: "How Can We Help the Poor?" After a moment's reflection the hen ventured, "I know what we can do! We can give them a ham and egg breakfast." "You can say that," the hog replied, "because for you that's just a contribution, but for me it's total commitment."

In sanctification God does not ask for a contribution; He asks for a commitment. The commitment that He wants is both an act and an attitude. It begins as a crisis and continues as a process.

General William Booth, founder of the Salvation Army, was once asked the reason for his spiritual power. He replied, "God has had all there is of me." This involved more than a casual giving; it was a total commitment. It involved an act of consecration out of which arose a lifelong attitude of surrender to God. When informed that he was going blind, he said, "I have done what I could for

God with two eyes. Now I will do what I can without any eyes."

George Muller said, "There was a day when I died, utterly died, to George Muller," (and as he spoke, he bent lower and lower until he almost touched the floor), "to his opinions, preferences, tastes, and will; died to the world, its approval or blame of even my brothers and friends. Since then I have studied to show myself approved only unto God." Was this a mere contribution? No, this was commitment, *total* commitment.

The death to self one experiences in the crisis of entire sanctification is to find extension in the "lived-out "death of a consecrated life. It is to die to self in order to live for God. The consequence of consecration is a kind of martyrdom on the installment plan—a daily living out of that consecration. This was the essence of Paul's plea to the Romans: "Present your bodies a living sacrifice, holy, acceptable unto God, which is your reasonable service." (Rom. 12:1).

Throughout history God has had His martyrs— persons whose lives were *taken* for the cause of Christ. But His greatest need is for living martyrs —persons whose lives are *given* in daily service

for the cause of Christ. May God enable us to sing
with Frances R. Havergal:

> *Take my will and make it Thine;*
> *It shall be no longer mine.*
> *Take my heart; it is Thine own;*
> *It shall be Thy royal throne.*
>
> *Take my love; my God, I pour*
> *At Thy fee its treasure store.*
> *Take myself and I will be*
> *Ever, only, all for Thee.*

COMETS AND STARS

Samuel Butler said that a certain person "proved to be a comet and no fixed star at all." There are many persons who, like a comet, make a bright, quick flash and then disappear from sight. It often happens in the sports world. Today's sensation is tomorrow's forgotten statistic. Comets flash and then fade, but the fixed stars shine steadily on.

Churches can also have comets and fixed stars. The comets make a dazzling display and then disappear. The fixed stars stay, and pray, and pay. They can be counted on. They are consistent. They do not call attention to themselves, as do the comets; rather, they give a steady light to a darkened world. The passing of time does not dim their glow. The seasons do not affect them. Winter, spring, summer, or fall, they are there on the job.

The Apostle Paul had converts of both types: comets and fixed stars. In his Epistles he referred to both, but his deep joy was for the fixed stars that God gave him. They were the ones he remembered with great satisfaction. They were the ones he prayed for and who prayed for him. They were the ones he longed to see. They were the ones he trusted with his young churches during prolonged absences from them.

Christians are to be shining lights in a darkened world. Jesus said, "Let your light so shine before men, that they may see your good works, and glorify your Father which is in heaven." (Matt. 5:16). Note that Jesus said others were to see our good works, not ourselves. He also said that when others saw our good works they would glorify God, not ourselves. Stars, not comets, are what God wants and needs.

The true Christian life cannot be lived out by the comet-type of person. While we delight in the brilliance of a dazzling conversion, the true test of faith is a lived-out life of daily devotion.

FAITH IN THE FIRE

The Bible tells of three youths who were known as "the three Hebrew children." Their faith put them in the fire. Their names were Shadrach, Meshach, and Abednego.

The king had issued a decree that, at the sound of the music, all must fall down and worship his image. To these young men this was unthinkable. They had early learned to serve the true and living God. So, in spite of the penalty for nonconformity (death in the fiery furnace), they stood erect when everyone else bowed. Word of this disrespect for a royal decree rapidly reached the king, who summoned the young men before him. Charged with the "crime," they promptly pleaded guilty and were sentenced to death.

The young men were given a chance to speak before they were executed. What a speech they made! They said to the king, "Our God is able to deliver us from the burning, fiery furnace." Their faith was being tested. It was the ultimate testing, for their very lives were at stake. "Faith," said William Newton Clark, "is daring the soul to go farther than it can see." These youths could not see the outcome of their act, but their faith assured them that God was able to preserve them. Theirs was a faith strong enough to believe that God could do the impossible.

Here is the proof of their commitment to God: They were willing to wrap their lives around their faith. They believed God was able to save them; but if He chose otherwise, they still would not worship the idol. They said, "But if not [if God did not deliver] . . . we will not serve thy gods." (Dan. 3:18). They were ready to accept God's will even if it went against their well-being. Sherwood Eddy said, "Faith is not trying to believe something regardless of the evidence. Faith is daring to do something regardless of the consequences." These youths felt that right was right whether they got burned or not.

Faithlessness cannot produce this kind of poise under pressure. The easy thing would have been to junk their faith and go the way of least resistance. They were a minority group in a foreign land, far removed from their own people and the place of their early training. Lesser souls might have taken the easy way out, but these youths were true to their heritage and to their God. Like their fellow captive, Daniel, who "purposed in his heart that he would not defile himself," they determined to hold to their convictions. They refused to take on the color of their new environment. They were not moral chameleons. Theirs was the kind of faith of which E.M. Wadsworth spoke: faith that would not shrink though washed in the waters of affliction.

Refusing to recant, the youths were bound after the sentence was passed and they were thrown into the furnace that was heated seven times hotter than ever before. Later, peering in to view the remains of the youths, the king was startled to see four live persons instead of three charred corpses. Four? Were not only three thrown into the furnace? Yes, but their number had increased, and the fourth was "like the Son of God." God was with them and they had suffered no hurt. Here is the biblical record: The fire had not destroyed them, not a hair had been singed, their coats had not been changed, and there was no smell of smoke on them. What a difference the presence of God made!

The story does not end there. The last verse of that account ends with this terse but telling statement: "Then the king promoted Shadrach, Meshach, and Abed-nego." Faith won. It always does.

DOWN, NOT OUT

As a boy, Stonewall Jackson was not a great fighter, but he did have a lot of grit and determination. A boyhood friend of his said, "I could throw him four times out of five, but he wouldn't stay *throwed*." Therein lay the secret of his success—persistence in spite of problems.

Life will throw us, but it is our job, by God's grace, not to "*stay throwed*." It is a fallacy to think that the Christian will not experience trials—even of the worst kind. Hebrews 11 is a record of God's greats who were thrown but who refused to give up. They refused to stay down. The Apostle Paul suffered a series of sorrows: scourging, stoning, beating, shipwreck, flood, robbery, peril at the hands of his own people as well as foreigners. (2 Cor. 11:23-27). But he wouldn't stay down.

Even our sinless Saviour knew the pangs of sorrow. "Though he were a Son, yet learned he obedience by the things which he suffered." (Heb. 5:8). Our Lord was despised, rejected, mocked, abused, crucified, and buried.

But He didn't stay down. On Easter morning the

mighty, resurrecting power of God released our Lord from the worst the world could do to Him.

Loss, disappointment, hurt and bereavement will come and even throw us temporarily. The Christian will experience the hurts that are common to mankind. But *being* thrown does not mean that we have to *stay* thrown. We have the assurance that God's grace is accessible to us when we need it. While flat on our backs, thrown by a mighty onslaught of perplexities, God's promise is that His grace is sufficient for us. (2 Cor. 12:9).

These lines from a much-beloved hymn should comfort us when life has gotten us down:

> *God hath not promised skies always blue,*
> *Flower-strewn pathways all our lives thro';*
> *God hath not promised sun without rain,*
> *Joy without sorrow, peace without pain.*

> *But God hath promised strength for the day,*
> *Rest for the labor, light for the way.*
> *Grace for the trials, help from above,*
> *Unfailing sympathy, undying love.*
> —ANNIE JOHNSON FLINT

NO PAST, NO FUTURE

Environmentalists and ecologists warn that America is rapidly becoming a nation without a past. By this they mean that many historical landmarks are being razed in order to create space for housing developments, super-highways, skyscrapers and open-pit mines. In the name of progress, historical sites and areas are being bulldozed so that the purposes of one of our latest and most revered gods—development—can be served.

Not only are our nation's landmarks being threatened. The cultures that flourished on this soil prior to the landing of the Pilgrims are in jeopardy. Many Indian burial sites, hunting grounds and worship centers have surrendered to the great, yellow Caterpillars with their deadly blades.

Developers gladly topple trees and replace them with black power poles in order to expand. "Progress" topples historical sites as readily as it topples trees.

A nation without a past. Sad, isn't it? Sadder still is a nation without a future. The big blade of progress which is separating us from the past, however, is a distant second to the spirit of godlessness which is separating us from our future. The Bible says the nations which forget God shall be turned into hell. (Ps. 9:17).

Our nation is in a period of godlessness which has been unequalled in our short history. The prevalence of corruption in government, bribery, perjury, tax evasion, wickedness in high places, plus decaying sex codes, alcoholism and drug abuse should warn us that such a forgetting of God carries with it the awesome penalty of an unrealized future.

Our nation was founded on the principles of righteousness. What a glorious past! But many of those principles have been bulldozed as readily as the sites on which they were founded. Let us be warned: A nation which loses such a past can also lose its future.

While God clearly warns of the annihilation that is imminent for a nation which forgets Him. He is also clear in telling what a nation can do to reverse its direction from a destiny of destruction. God says, "If my people, which are called by my name, shall humble themselves, and pray, and seek my face, and turn from their wicked ways; then will I hear from heaven, and will forgive their sin, and will heal their land." (2 Chron. 7:14). America's present need is for such a healing. Only then can she have a future.

CLOUDS AND DUST

One day in our younger years, my brothers and I saw a huge golden eagle standing in a plowed field. His head drooped and his wings were dragging the ground. He made little effort to escape as we approached. Something was obviously wrong with him. At first glance he appeared to be a perfect specimen; however, closer examination revealed his problem. In the joint of one of his great wings a disease had eaten away the flesh and muscles, making him incapable of flying.

God had made him for the clouds, but disease reduced him to the dust. Made to soar in the heavens, his disease caused him to share the habitat of gophers and ground squirrels.

Sin does the same thing to man. Made in the image of God, created only a little lower than the angels, man is destined for the heights. But sin changes the designs of Deity and brings man down to the depths. Like a deadly disease, sin eats away at the soul until one is only a shell of what God intended him to be. Like a handless glove, he has shape but not substance. Hollow and helpless, he is a pawn of Satan, ready for sin to do its final work. Sin, when it is finished, brings forth death, the Bible says. (Jas. 1:15).

Only Christ has the power to purge sin from man's soul, set his spirit free, and send him soaring. In his great hymn "And Can It Be," Charles Wesley states the redemption theme beautifully in these words:

> *Long my imprisoned spirit lay,*
> *Fast bound in sin and nature's night.*
> *Thine eyes diffused a quickening ray.*
> *I woke; the dungeon flamed with light.*
> *My chains fell off; my heart was free.*
> *I rose, went forth, and followed Thee.*

Man is made for the clouds, not the dust. Sin would reverse that, but grace enables man to rise to the heights for which he was created.

THE CURSE OF CONFORMITY

To some degree, all persons are conformists. Man, a gregarious creature, seeks to behave in ways that will gain the approval of his fellows. Wishing to be like others, he gives attention to customs, styles of dress and patterns of speech and behavior.

The call to conform is a strong social force which can have ethical implications. Society demands conformity, including ethical conformity. E. Stanley Jones said, "If you fall beneath its standards it will punish you; if you rise above its standards it will persecute you." The result of such ethical conformity is a moral in-betweenness, making one a blurred face in the big crowd. The social force exerted upon one is to be neither too bad nor too good.

Conformity can become a curse when it concerns character. The tendency to explain questionable ethics by the maxim "Everybody's doing it" is a lame excuse. William Ward said, "Character is always lost when a high ideal is sacrificed on the altars of conformity and popularity." When conformity is at the cost of character, the price is too great.

Emerson said, "Whoso would be a man must be a nonconformist." That is especially so for the man who is in Christ. His call to us is to deny ourselves and take up our cross and follow Him. (Matt. 16:24). Sometimes this self-denial will be the most difficult at the point of wanting to please men. But if our desire is for higher values—to please God-it may call for non-conformity.

Some have believed that to be Christian they must be odd (and they have been eminently successful in developing that fallacy!). To be a Christian, however, means that one will not be odd but different. The difference is the grace of God operating freely within, making him like Christ and unlike the world.

This is what Paul had in mind when he wrote to the Romans: "Don't let the world around you squeeze you into its own mold." (Rom. 12:2, Phillips). Conformity to Christ assures us that we will not become conformed to the world.

ADVERSITY

Adversity makes some persons bitter. It makes others better. The difference is the attitude that is taken toward it.

Simply stated, adversity is trouble. Christians and non-Christians alike experience it. It is said that some people have three kinds of trouble at once: (1) all they have ever had, (2) all they have at present, and (3) all they ever expect to have. This last—anticipating adversity—is commonly known as "borrowing trouble." Jesus said that borrowing trouble is not necessary because each day has enough troubles of its own. (Matt. 6:34).

Josh Billings said, "Life is a grindstone, and whether it grinds a man down or polishes him up depends on the stuff he's made of." The character of the individual, plus the view one has of himself and the world around him, determines how he will react to adversity. Springett said, "No sorrow leaves us where it found us; it drives us from God or brings us nearer to him." The difference is in the person, not the problem.

Adversity can aid in developing strength for coping with the routines of life. *Front Rank* reported that on one occasion a man on a nature hunt found the cocoon of an emperor moth from which the imprisoned insect was just about to emerge. Wanting to add the moth to his collection, he watched for it to leave the cocoon. Soon the moth began struggling as it tried to get out through a tiny hole in the cocoon. Desiring to aid it, the man enlarged the hole and the moth crawled out and dropped helplessly to the ground, never to fly. The would-be helper learned later that struggle forces strength into a moth's wings. Without the struggle it can never become airborne.

It is known that the hardest wood is found at timberline. There the trees have to withstand blizzards of winter and the blasts of thousands of gales in order to survive. It is said that the tight grain of wood from timberline produces the best tones for violins. The struggle to survive builds a quality into the wood that produces beautiful music.

Adversity can produce both strength and beauty in the Christian's life. This is what the Apostle Paul meant when he said that our temporary, light affliction produces for us an "eternal weight of glory." (2 Cor. 4:17). Instead of working against us, trouble can work for us. Its function is to make us better, not bitter.

GAIN AND GODLINESS

There is no necessary conflict between gain and godliness. They are not mutually exclusive, nor must one choose between them. Without doubt, however, it is most difficult to have both riches and righteousness. The Bible has much to say about the dangers of materialism.

There can be no doubt that materialism has a strong, addictive power. The Apostle Paul said that those who *crave to be rich* fall into temptation and a snare. (1 Tim. 6:9). Not only the wealthy but the would-be wealthy run the risk of ruination by riches.

Materialism can be spiritually deadly. Because of it, some Christians have erred from the faith and have been pierced with many sorrows. Greed plunges one into the lusts that drown men in destruction. The matter is dealt with decisively and directly by Paul when he says that "the love of money is a root of all kinds of evil." (1 Tim. 6:10, NIV).

Over against the greed for gain is the goal of godliness. The focus on gain is on this world; the focus on godliness is on the world to come. Pity the man who plans for one world and who, as it ends, finds there is another for which he is not prepared. The Bible instructs us to lay hold on to eternal life. (v. 12). If we must be greedy and grasping, let us grasp hold of eternal life. If we would seek for godliness as earnestly as we seek for gain, how rich we would be!

Scripture confronts us with the practical logic of placing the focus on godliness and not gain: "We brought nothing into this world, and it is certain we can carry nothing out." (v. 7). Saladin, the Moslem conqueror, dramatized this truth by directing his followers to bury him with his hands sticking out of the grave to show that eternity is entered empty-handed.

There is truth in the maxim, "You can't take it with you." But if the Christian lays up treasures in heaven, his riches will be there when he arrives.

"DEAR GOD, WHAT CAN I DO FOR YOU?"

A little girl finished her prayer by saying, "And now, dear God, what can I do for You?" In spite of her years, she was spiritually mature enough to see the other side of prayer, that *getting from* God is to be balanced by *giving to* God.

There is nothing wrong in asking God for things. Our Lord himself told us to ask His Father for things. ("daily bread"). But this does not mean that asking is to be the whole of praying. In fact, prayers that major on asking God for things reflect a self-centered, spiritually neurotic personality concerned only with one's own wishes and desires.

It is fortunate for us that God does not always give us what we want. He has committed himself to take care of our needs, but He has not promised to pamper our whims. A child who is showered with gifts and attention becomes both unappreciative and unconcerned for others. God wants no spoiled children. Our Heavenly Father seeks to save us from the snare of selfishness by helping us to balance receiving *from* Him with responding *to* Him. As physical life is sustained by inhaling and exhaling, so spiritual life is maintained by receiving and giving.

If we would end our prayer with "Now, dear God, what can I do for You?" He would perhaps show us the following:

1. That we can best express our love to Him by serving others. Jesus said that a kindness done to one of the least of His brothers is a kindness done to Him. Christianity cannot be divorced from human personality. Christianity is *for* persons and is expressed *to* persons.

2. That we can show our love for Him by caring for the concerns of His Church. Does not the Church for which Christ gave His life merit our loving service?

3. That much receiving demands much responding. "Freely ye have received, freely give" is the injunction of Christ to His disciples.

4. That "repayment" of His love can be done only in token form. Whatever we do for Him only recognizes our debt; it never pays it. Let us ask God what we can do for Him in response to His immeasurable love for us.

TRASH AND TREASURE

A store in the Ozarks carries the interesting name Trash Treasure. It is not hard to imagine what kind of business it is. It is a store that is filled with hundreds of wares ranging from the ridiculous to the rare. The buyer is on his own to determine which wares are trash and which are treasure.

Life is like that, isn't it? It is filled with all kinds of things and it is our responsibility to find the things of worth among the worthless. But unlike buyers in a trash and treasure store, Christians are not on their own in making choices of life. We can be guided by some basic principles which will help us make the right choices.

The surest Guide for knowing the difference between trash and treasure is God's Word. When we utilize God's Word in the choices of life, we save ourselves from the snares of subjectivity to which we are so susceptible. Applying the test of the Bible enables us to see through the eyes of God, so that we can "live with eternity's values in view."

Another way of knowing the difference between

trash and treasure is to seek earnestly and prayerfully for the guidance of the Holy Spirit. The Holy Spirit is never contrary to the Word of God. A "leading of the Holy Spirit" which violates the Word of God is neither a leading nor an evidence of the Holy Spirit. God does not contradict himself.

Still another way of telling trash from treasure is to apply this test: What would Christ choose under these circumstances? Our Lord himself used the principles of God's Word and the Spirit's leading in His own life; thus He is our best Example in showing us how to determine the difference between the worthless and the worthwhile.

NONE IS PLENTY

On returning from a safari in India, a hunter reported to a friend that he had not killed a tiger. When asked if this was a great disappointment, the hunter replied, "No, when you are hunting for tigers, none is plenty."

Let us look at some aspects of church life where none is enough.

None is plenty with regard to the number of people who are unwilling to work for Christ and His Church. It is most unfortunate that, in church after church, a large percent of the work is done by a small percent of the membership.

Someone has said that the church is filled with willing people—a few willing to work and the rest willing to let them. That is too true to be humorous. It takes many people doing many things for a church to maintain a vibrant, meaningful ministry. The degree of noninvolvement is a measure of the church's ineffectiveness.

A second case where none is plenty is the number of pessimists in a local congregation (worse yet, on a church board). It has been said that an optimist sees opportunities in difficulties but a pessimist sees difficulties in opportunities. Generally speaking, pessimists are generally speaking; thus they spread their gloom in amounts disproportionate to their number.

Sometimes pessimism goes under the guise of caution, giving it a cloak of respectability. While a case should not be made for reckless abandon, let it be said that fewer churches suffer from unbounded enthusiasm than from unrestrained pessimism.

A church that is going, growing, and glowing is one that has refused to believe the minority report that gloomily states, "It can't be done."

Finally, none is plenty when it comes to people with a critical spirit. A judgmental attitude is diametrically opposed to the teachings of Jesus as well as to the spirit of the entire New Testament. Notwithstanding, persons can be found in many churches who feel constrained to criticize the pastor, the people, and the program. One who does so fails to realize that he reveals more of his own faults than he exposes in that which he criticizes.

Let us examine ourselves and see if we are making some negative contributions which our church could do without.

A WORD TO WORRYWARTS

Thomas Carlyle had a neighbor whose rooster invariably awakened him at dawn by its loud crowing. Carlyle protested to this neighbor about the annoyance. The man reminded him that the rooster crowed only three or four times.

"That may be true," replied Carlyle, "but if you could only know what I go through while waiting for him to crow!"

Some people compound present problems by anticipating future ones. There is a rather impressive psychiatric term which describes the behavior of persons with this problem. It is called *psychasthenia*. In common usage this kind of person is called, indelicately, a worrywart.

Jesus had this to say to worrywarts: "Take therefore no thought for the morrow: for the morrow shall take thought for the things of itself. Sufficient unto the day is the evil thereof." (Matt. 6:34). He meant that each day has enough troubles of its own without worrying about tomorrow's troubles.

The human organism has been designed by Deity to handle a reasonable amount of stress and tension. But chronic worry "overloads the circuits," and one's psychic energy is used up too rapidly. This abuse of psychic energy leaves one without the needed reserves for creative, wholesome living.

Much physical suffering can be attributed to excessive worry. When one's inner resources are depleted, the organism then becomes an easy prey to a variety of debilitating physical ills. Our Lord knew this full well, and that is why He warned us about the dangers of worry. Would not the Lord, who created us, know the limits of the human organism?

Perhaps we should let the following prayer by Peter Marshall become ours: "Help us to do our best this day and be content with today's troubles, so that we shall not borrow the troubles of tomorrow. Save us from the sin of worrying, lest stomach ulcers be the badge of our lack of faith. Amen." Amen!

KNOWING WHERE TO STOP

A second grader came home from his school's track and field day proudly displaying a beautiful blue ribbon. When asked what race he won, he replied, "I didn't win a race. I got the ribbon for stopping at the right place."

Of all of the boys in the race, he was the only one who followed directions and ran by the rules. A blue ribbon for knowing where to stop!

If God gives honors to those who win, surely He must also give blue ribbons to His children who know where to stop. Consider these situations in Christian living when knowing where to stop is important.

1. Stop before talk becomes gossip. It takes a great deal of discernment to determine where talk ends and gossip begins. Talk can be harmless, but it can also lead to gossip before one is scarcely aware of it. Plautus suggested this sure cure for gossiping: "All tattlers should be hanged by their tongues, and those who listen to them should be hanged by their ears."

Several men were engaged in conversation about a mutual acquaintance who was experiencing spiritual difficulty. One asked another how the man in question was getting along. His reply was magnificent in its Christian simplicity: "He needs our prayers."

His reply was calculated to do two things: (a) to end a discussion which could have been damaging, and (b) to enlist support in place of judgment. He knew where to stop.

2. Stop before concern becomes worry. Sometimes we assume we are "carrying a burden" when, in fact, we are worrying. A huge sign on a church in Denver twists a phrase by asking: "Why pray when you can worry?"

Concern and worry feel much the same, but they are quite different. Knowing where to stop leads to a life of trust instead of a life of tension.

3. Stop before disappointment becomes bitterness. Life has its disappointments. They are common to all persons. While we cannot always choose what happens to us, we can, by God's grace, choose our attitudes toward what happens to us. Blue ribbons should be given to those who know where to stop. Have you been winning any lately?

SERVICE

The great violinist, Nicolo Paganini, willed his beautiful and valuable instrument to his native city of Genoa. A condition of the will was that the violin was not to be used. This was a most unfortunate stipulation, for a peculiarity of wood is that as long as it is used, it wears only slightly; but as soon as it is discarded, it begins to decay.

Paganini's violin has become worm-eaten and without value except as a relic. This should teach us something about the nature of service.

Albert Pike said, "What we have done for ourselves alone, dies with us; what we have done for others and the world, remains and is immortal." Not only does service for others take on a measure of immortality; it also brings meaning and value to one's life in the present.

Dr. Albert Schweitzer, whose entire life was characterized by service, said, "I don't know what your destiny will be, but one thing I know: The only ones among you who will be really happy are those who will have sought and found how to serve."

Every Christian is afforded the opportunity for service. It is a wide-open door to anyone who will enter it. Jesus taught us how to serve. He gave the world its greatest object lesson on service when He died on the Cross. The Crucifixion was history's most selfless act.

But this does not mean that service is limited to the great and spectacular. Did Jesus not tell us that even the gift of a cup of cold water was itself an act of service? (Matt. 10:42)

The motivating force for service is love. Indeed, love and service are inseparably linked together. John Oxenham wrote:

> *Love ever gives—*
> *Forgives, outlives—*
> *And ever stands with open hands.*
> *And while it lives, it gives,*
> *For this is love's prerogative—*
> *To give, and give, and give.*

Some time ago *Guideposts* recounted an incident in the life of John Ruskin. As he sat with a friend at a window one evening, they watched a lamplighter's torch ignite the streetlamps on a distant hill. Darkness obscured the lamplighter, but his progress could be observed as successive lamps were lighted.

Ruskin said, "That illustrates what I mean by a genuine Christian. You may not know him or even see him, but his way has been marked by the lights he leaves burning."

THE GRASSHOPPER COMPLEX (Part I)

Ten of the 12 spies who scouted out the land of Canaan were convinced that it could not be taken. They were suffering from a "grasshopper complex." Seeing the giants in Canaan, they reported, "We were in our own sight as grasshoppers." (Num. 13:33). They were suffering from a low self-concept, a distorted self-image.

Their assignment by Moses was not to see *if* the land could be taken but *how* it was to be taken. The *if* was settled centuries earlier when God promised them the land in His covenant to their forefather Abraham. The *how* was the human element in the divine-human enterprise.

Their report was both good and bad: It was a good land flowing with milk and honey; and the grapes, figs, and pomegranates were delicious. But there were giants in the land! Compared with the giants, they felt like grasshoppers.

Their low self-concept was not only a self-imposed insult; it was also an injustice to God. Certainly it was no credit to the Creator, in whose image they were fashioned, to view themselves as insects.

The spirit of the 10 spies still lives in the ranks of God's people. Countless persons in the Church suffer from a low self-concept. They view themselves as less than they are and most certainly as less than they could be.

This poor self-image often goes under the guise of humility. But it is a false humility which labels oneself as less than God made him. Genuine humility is the art of seeing oneself as he is, not as less than he is.

The grasshopper complex can become an excuse for low-level living. Seeking to excuse his questionable behavior, a parishioner explained, "I'm only a weak worm of the dust, you know."
His pastor replied, "Yes, and if you are not careful, the devil will pick you up and go fishing with you!"

The grasshopper complex can also become an excellent excuse for not engaging in the work of the Lord. Many jobs go begging in the church because persons with a low self-concept say, "I could never do a job that big." As a consequence, the church goes limping along while some of her members go hopping off.

THE GRASSHOPPER COMPLEX (Part II)

The 10 spies who brought back an evil report from the land of Canaan felt that it could not be conquered because it was inhabited by giants. Not only did they report that they felt like grasshoppers themselves, but "so we were in their sight." (Num. 13:33).

Now who told those 10 spies that the giants viewed them as grasshoppers? Surely it was not the giants. Spies are not accustomed to chatting openly with the enemy. Besides, it is not likely they spoke the same language, even if they were of a disposition to engage in such a conversation.

No, the 10 spies got their notions of the giant's appraisal of them from their own low self-concept. Because the spies saw themselves as grasshoppers, they assumed that others saw them as such. It is a common error to assume that others view us as we view ourselves.

It's bad to see oneself as a grasshopper. The disaster is doubled when one assumes that others see him as such. It becomes debilitating. That is what happened to the 10 spies. To assume that the

Israelites could overthrow the sons of Anak-that grasshoppers could whip giants—was a bit too much for their imagination.

How quickly they had forgotten the marvelous intervention of God in their recent past—their emancipation from Pharaoh, and the Lord's parting of the waters of the Red Sea so that they could be on their way to the Promised Land!

The 10 spies were so occupied with visions of their smallness that they failed to remember God's greatness. Having done so, they brought back an evil report, and caused God's people to wander 40 years in the wilderness.

A vision of our smallness and a lack of vision of God's greatness can combine to block the work of God in any age. Let us move forward to "possess the land" and let God take care of the giants. And let us get our view of our worth, not from ourselves, or from others, but from the Creator who made us in His own image.

HELPING PEOPLE CRY

Landis Rogers tells of a six-year old girl who was sent to a neighborhood grocery for a loaf of bread. The errand took longer than necessary, so her mother asked why she was delayed.

The little girl said that she had met her friend. Susie, who had broken her doll. Her mother said, "Did you stay that long because you were helping Susie fix it?"

"No, Mother, that's not what kept me so long. I was helping her cry."

What a beautiful statement! What the little girl did was to show empathy. Empathy is not the same as sympathy. Sympathy is feeling sorry *for* someone. Empathy is feeling sorry *with* someone. Empathy has been defined as "your ache in my heart."

Henry David Thoreau said that most men live lives of quiet desperation. For many this desperation is the desperation of loneliness, of feeling that no one cares for them. It has been said that there is more hunger for love in the world than there is hunger for bread. That is a very broad statement, but it is true nonetheless.

Dr. Paul Tournier, the respected Christian

psychotherapist, said that no one can find a full life without feeling understood by at least one person. How true that is! As Christians we have the opportunity and responsibility of being friends to the friendless and of crying with those who cry.

One said of his friend, "When I met him, I was looking down. When I left him, I was looking up." What had his friend done? The friend had identified with him so completely that his spirit was lifted, and his life took on a brighter hue. A beautiful Japanese proverb says, "One kind word can warm three winter months."

Every Christian is called into the ministry of caring. It is a ministry that our Lord himself has showed us how to perform. In the Gospels, mention is often made of the compassion of Jesus. Compassion—empathy—characterized His entire life, and it should characterize ours.

Christ taught us the necessity of empathy in the golden rule: "Whatsoever ye would that men should do to you, do ye even so to them." (Matt. 7:12). This can be paraphrased as follows: "Do unto others as though you were the others."

May God help us to "rejoice with them that do rejoice, and weep with them that weep." (Rom. 12:15). That is empathy.

BETWEEN BIRTH AND DEATH

Entering a hospital to call on a parishioner, I became aware of a flurry of excitement coming from the maternity ward of the hospital. Curious, I walked that direction and heard music being played by a five-piece band in the corridor outside the room of a new mother. Her husband, thrilled that he was a father, had arranged for the band to serenade his wife

.

It seemed a bit incongruous, that kind of activity in that kind of setting. In place of the usual quiet, austere efficiency could be heard festive music provided by a man who was delighted that his child had been born. All normal activity ceased, and people of all kinds—orderlies, nurses, doctors, and visitors—were captivated by what was taking place. All of us shared the warmth of this loving gesture.

The maternity ward is the happiest place in the hospital. There one feels that he has a kinship with the ages, that he is linked to the distant past as well as to the future. He feels that he is viewing the ongoingness of life. As Carl Sandburg said, "A baby is God's opinion that the world should go on."

As I was basking in the glow of this warm, human experience, a nurse's aide, who recognized me, asked if I knew Mary Brown. I told her that I didn't know Mary but that I did know some of her family. The nurse's aide told me that Mary was a patient upstairs, very ill, and that she would be grateful if I visited her.

As I made my way to her room, I began fitting together bits of information that I knew about her. She was 28, had lived most of her life in poverty, and was married to a man who made life so frighteningly miserable for her that she was forced to leave him for her own safety. Now she was desperately ill in the large, lonely city. All of this was running through my mind as I walked through the door to her room. The room was empty. On checking at the nurses' station, I learned that Mary had died a short time before. As far as I know, she died alone. No one—parents, husband, or even her friend downstairs—was there when she died.

I cannot adequately express the mixed emotions I had on that occasion. Downstairs in the maternity ward was to be found the throbbing of life; on the floor above was the pall of death. By chance I came into both situations only moments apart. One life had come into the world to the strains of music and the warmth of love, and another life had gone out of the world in stark loneliness and cold unconcern.

I finished my calling and left the hospital, trying to grasp the significance of that moving experience. I came to these conclusions: (1) It doesn't *really* matter under what conditions we are born; (2) it doesn't *really* matter under what conditions we die; but (3) it *does* matter the kind of life which we live.

While none of us had a choice in determining the conditions under which he would be born, and none of us will be able to arrange the conditions under which he will die, all of us can select the principles, by which we will live. In our quest for these life principles, it is impossible to improve on the example which Christ set for us. He, like that baby, was born to the strains of music, and like the young woman, died in aloneness and unconcern. But between those great moments, His life was lived with a driving passion to do His Father's will. This absorbed His every waking moment. We can do likewise!

An example of this philosophy was Dr. Paul Carlson, the young medical missionary who was martyred in November, 1964, in the Congo. Who is to say that he died before his time? He lived to do his Father's will, and he did it. Is there any improvement on that? Consider Jim Elliot and his missionary companions who were martyred for the cause of Christ in Ecuador in the mid-fifties. Were their lives wasted? History, even at this early date, says emphatically, "No, they were *not* wasted." Why? Because on the very spot where they gave their lives, the work of missions now flourishes.

Between birth and death there is a life to be lived. That life, however short or long, can best be lived as we give ourselves to Christ in service to others. May we pledge with Charles Wesley:

> *To serve the present age,*
> *My calling to fulfil;*
> *Oh, may it all my powers engage*
> *To do my Master's will.*

THE BODY: SERVANT OR MASTER?

A young man said to his counselor, "I have discovered that I have been taking orders from my body, that I have been doing what my body felt like doing. Now I have decided that my body is going to be my servant and that it is going to take orders from me."

What a great insight! It is an insight which will be life-changing for that person. When one learns to make his body his servant, not his master, he is released to enter an era of productivity he has not previously known.

For centuries many have believed that the body is inherently evil. Fortunately, that era has passed. But while it is no longer commonly held that the body is inherently evil, it is well known that one's body can be one of his greatest enemies. It can be his enemy if he does only what his body feels like doing. Many times the body feels like doing nothing. One person expressed it this way:

One fierce ambition consumes me wholly,
Doing nothing, very slowly!

A good question for the Christian to ask himself is this: To what extent has my body governed me when I worked for Christ and determined how much service I have performed? An honest appraisal will probably reveal that often much was left undone because one did not *feel* like doing it at the time. It might be staggering to know how many services were missed, how many Sunday school lessons were not studied, and how many missions of mercy were not made, simply because persons did not *feel* like doing those things at the time.

Psychiatrists, psychologists, and counsellors are keenly aware of the relationship between physical activity and mental health. These persons know the value of getting the mentally depressed person into physical activity. In some cases, mental depression can be lifted through physical activity alone.

What if the great characters of the Bible had been persons who took orders from their bodies? Undoubtedly, their accomplishments would not have been so great. Consider the "greats" of faith recorded in Hebrews 11. Can it be supposed that they all felt like doing what they did? Probably not. After all, who does *feel* like stopping the mouths of lions, being stoned to death, or being sawed in two? Undoubtedly, Paul and Silas did not *feel* like praying and singing praise to God at midnight in jail at Philippi, but they did. Assuredly,

Jesus did not *feel* like going to the Cross (and don't forget Gethsemane), but He did. All of these, and a host of others, lived by the principle that the body is the servant, not the master.

Living by this great insight will result in the following:

1. It will release the Christian to do a host of worthwhile activities which would otherwise not get done.

2. It will promote better mental health in the person who is prone to be body-oriented.

3. It will help to take Christianity out of the realm of feeling and place it in the realm of the will, which is its proper domain.

4. It will advance the kingdom of God.

Let us examine our lives to determine if we are permitting our bodies to be barriers to the advancement of the Kingdom. God has given us our bodies to further His work, not hinder it.

THE TIMELESS CHURCH

The Church predates the world, and it will postdate the world. Before the foundations of the world were set, God chose His Church. After man's last clock has stopped, the Church will still exist. The Church was conceived by God the Father; it was given birth by Christ, the Son; and it is being nurtured by God the Holy Spirit. The Church is before time, above time, and beyond time. Time did not create the Church, nor can time destroy it. It is so strong that the very gates of hell cannot withstand it. It is so invincible that, after Satan's worst is done to it, it will come through without spot or wrinkle.

Jude paints a portrait of God as the Protector and Sustainer of the Church. While Satan is doing all in his power to destroy the Church, God is there to give both protection and sustenance to the Church. Jude gives us this grand assurance: He "is able to keep you from falling." When Jude saw the great contrast between the awfulness of sin and the greatness of God, it is no wonder that he concluded, "To the only wise God our Saviour, be glory and majesty, dominion and power, both now and ever. Amen."

As Christians we are not only a part of the Church —we *are* the church. The Church is not a place where Christians go; the Church is what Christians are. What a holy honor, what a priceless privilege, what a real responsibility to be members of the timeless Church!

Those things which we call "ours" will some day be taken from us—our homes, our cars, our possessions. They cannot last because they are subject to the ravages of time. The familiar motto which is seen in many homes says:

> *Only one life, 'twill soon be past;*
> *Only what's done for Christ will last.*

There is a profound truth in that motto. That being so, let us invest our lives in Christ's timeless Church. It alone will survive the centuries.

GUARDING THE CHURCH

Christ died for the Church. Anything worth dying for is worth preserving and building. This, then, is what God has called us to do—to preserve and build the Church for which Christ gave His life.

The Church has always been in double jeopardy: (1) There are outside foes that would destroy it; and (2) there are inside foes that would destroy it. The foes outside the Church are readily discernible because they are wolves in wolves' clothing. It is the inside foes that post the greatest threat to the Church because they are wolves in sheep's clothing.

It is said that a certain tree on the slopes of Long's Peak in the Colorado Rockies survived being struck by lightning 14 times, only to meet its death by an innocent looking, tiny insect which attacked the tree from within.

John's Third Epistle tells of one of the Early Church's inside foes. His name was Diotrephes. He tried to cause dissension by refusing to entertain traveling missionaries. He threatened to put out of the church those who ignored his demands. Wicked action and insulting language were also attributed to him.

John clearly stated that this internal enemy was to be ignored and that the church was to continue doing the right. John was affirming the truth that the Church for which Christ died was to refuse to be sidetracked from its holy purpose.

In Acts 20:28-30 this call to guard the Church is crystal clear: "Take heed to yourselves and to all the flock, in which the Holy Spirit has made you guardians, to feed the church of the Lord which he obtained with his own blood. I know that after my departure fierce wolves will come in among you, not sparing the flock; and from among your own selves will arise men speaking perverse things, to draw away the disciples after them" (RSV). This passage warns of both the outside and inside foes of the Church. Against both the Church must be guarded.

Timothy Dwight expressed the Christian's loving concern for the Church in these words:

> *For her my tears shall fall;*
> *For her my prayers ascend;*
> *To her my cares and toils be given*
> *Till toils and cares shall end.*

THE UNITY OF THE CHURCH

The Church is the body of Christ, of which He is the Head. (Col. 1:19). A body cannot exist apart from the head. When the body and the head are severed, death results. This is also true of Christ and His Church.

The relationship between Christ and His Church must be viewed as a living relationship. Christianity is not static; it is dynamic. It is not a way of life; it *is* life. The Church is not a thing; it is an organism.

When Saul of Tarsus was on the way to Damascus to persecute the Church, Jesus accosted him and asked, "Why do you persecute me?" Saul had not been persecuting the person of Christ, but Christ's relationship to His Church was so close that what hurt the Church hurt Him. Likewise, when one member of the Church body is hurt, the whole body experiences pain. When a member of the physical body, let us say a hand, suffers a painful injury, it does not say to the body. "You go to sleep, and I'll stay awake and hurt." No, if the hand is in pain, the whole body knows it. That is the way it is with the Church, for it is a living organism.

John Fawcett expressed this thought in these lines:

We share our mutual woes,
Our mutual burdens bear;
And often for each other flows
The sympathizing tear.

In the Church we are not only one with each other; we are one with Christ. As our Head, He gives us our directions; as His body, we are channels through whom He does His work. This dual interrelatedness between the members of the Church and between its members and Christ forms the medium through which the purposes of Almighty God are accomplished in His world.

A "division" in the church is contrary to both its nature and purpose. As William Barclay says, if it becomes divided, it ceases to be the Church, and its work ceases. It is as incorrect to speak of a church as being divided against itself as it is to speak of a Christian as being divided from Christ. When a church ceases to be united, it ceases to be a church.

The Church is a unity of Head and body as well as a unity within the body. This unity is both its glory and its opportunity.

GOING SOMEWHERE

The processionary caterpillars instinctively travel in slow, nose-to-tail caravans through the trees on which they feed. A naturalist once lured a train of them onto the rim of a large flowerpot, making an unbroken circle of furry bodies. Devoid of a leader and deprived of a destination, they circled the pot for almost a week until they died of exhaustion and starvation.

That illustrates the plight of persons without Christ. Lacking a Leader and a purpose, people plod wearily through an endless circle of meaninglessness which culminates in spiritual deprivation and death.

Without Christ, men take an uncertain path toward an undefined goal. Some seem to be satisfied to substitute distance for direction—but like the hapless caterpillars, much going takes them nowhere. It is not the distance that one travels that matters. Rather, it is the direction in which one goes that is of ultimate importance.

When the Russians first achieved a manned space flight around the earth, one cynic observed, "Man is now capable of going in greater circles than ever before." While not disparaging the scientific genius of the feat, he was trying to point out that our greatest need is for direction, not distance.

Christ came to offer an option to such purposeless existence. The attractive alternative is meaningful purpose here, culminating in paradise hereafter. Christ declared that He is "The Way."—The Way that leads to happiness now and heaven later. He promised His people that He would prepare a place for them and that He would return and take them to that place. A Leader, a Way, and a destination— what more do we need? What more could we want?

A man was lost in the jungles of Burma. Finding a native, he asked, "Can you tell me the way out of this jungle?" As the native began clearing a path with his large knife, he replied, "There is no way, I am the way. Follow me."

That is Christ's message to man: "I am the Way. Follow Me and I will lead you out of the darkness into light and out of hopelessness into heaven."

RESURRECTION REFLECTIONS

The Resurrection has both divine and human dimensions. It was a divine act with human implications. When Christ was resurrected, His disciples were resurrected in their Christian living. Let us see what the Resurrection means to the Christian life as demonstrated in the lives of the disciples.

1. *The Resurrection replaces fear with faith.* At the Crucifixion, all of the disciples, save John, forsook Christ and fled. They became cowards behind locked doors. (John 20:19). But the Resurrection changed that! Faith was not only restored but amplified.

2. *The Resurrection relates conduct to creed.* The Resurrection did not change Christianity's creed; it verified it. It is a bogus Christianity that permits a great gap between creed and conduct, between belief and action. Luke 24:21 depicts the post-Crucifixion disappointment of the disciples: "We trusted that it had been he which should have redeemed Israel." They promptly went into spiritual retirement. But the Resurrection changed that, too!

3. *The Resurrection reduces death to delay.* At the

funeral of the saintly A.J. Gordon, Dr. A. T. Pierson told that he received the telegram announcing Dr. Gordon's death at three o'clock in the morning. Afterward, being unable to go back to sleep, he read the entire New Testament to see what it said about death.

He found that after the resurrection of Jesus, the apostles seldom used the word "death" to describe the close of a Christian's life. Rather, "asleep" was the common biblical substitute for the term "death." What comfort to view death as an interruption of life rather than its cessation! Clement said, "Christ has turned our sunsets into sunrise." The Resurrection accounts for that!

The Resurrection occurred centuries ago, but that ancient act of the Almighty has deep significance for Christian living today. The Resurrection was more than an event in history—it was an event that changed all of subsequent history. Let us face the future in the knowledge that our Lord's apparent defeat by His death was swallowed up in glorious victory by His resurrection.

Lift up your heads, ye sorrowing ones,
And be ye glad of heart,
For Calvary Day and Easter Day,
Earth's saddest day and gladdest day,
Were just one day apart!
—AUTHOR UNKNOWN

THRIVING ON NEGLECT

A plant nursery in California has a sign which reads, "Native trees and shrubs for sale. They thrive on neglect." That is a catchy come-on, isn't it? There is a certain appeal to the promise of having things of beauty and value that require no attention or cultivation.

While it may be possible to grow some trees and shrubs without giving attention to care and cultivation, a Christian character cannot grow under conditions of neglect.

In fact, nothing that is valuable in our lives can thrive on neglect. Neglect the body, and it will become sick or die. Neglect the mind, and it will become dull and lazy. Neglect the spirit, and it will become ill or warped.

We know this to be true, yet how subtle is the temptation to become neglectful-especially in the things of the spirit—while still hoping to thrive spiritually! Gladstone, the British statesman, was once asked if he believed in ghosts. He replied, "No, but I'm afraid of them!"

This points up the difference between believing and behaving. We do not always let our knowledge govern our actions. As a consequence, we permit ourselves to perform contrary to our perception.

Here are some things we cannot neglect:

1. We cannot neglect the prayer life and thrive as Christians. Samuel Logan Brengle said, "Know . . . that all failure has its beginning in the closet, in failing to pray."

2. We cannot neglect God's Word and thrive as Christians. Paul instructed Timothy to give attention to reading, reminding him that by giving attention to reading and doctrine he would save both himself and others. (1 Tim. 4:14-16).

3. We cannot be thriving Christians and neglect attending church. Samuel Shoemaker told of a pastor who called at the home of one of his members who had been absenting himself from church. As they sat by the fireplace, the pastor took the tongs and lifted a live coal from the fire and placed it on the hearth. Together they watched it die.

The member said, "You need not say a word, sir; I'll be there next Sunday." Let us determine not to follow the fallacy that we can thrive on neglect. Rather, let us give careful attention to the cultivation of Christian character.

WHAT CHRIST WANTS FOR CHRISTMAS

The trip from Nazareth had been long and arduous. Many miles they had travelled—Mary riding on the back of a donkey, and Joseph walking wearily beside her.

The tax decree from Caesar could not have come at a worse time for Mary. She was great with child and the trip had been exhausting.

At the journey's end the couple found that no room was available, so necessity forced them to seek shelter in a stable. "There was no room for them in the inn." There is irony in that statement. It was not rank strangers who would not give them a room; it was their own kinsmen.

Each town in Judea was filled with relatives, because the census decree required that persons must register in the city of their forefathers. Bethlehem was no exception. Thus when the earthly parents of Jesus were forced to find refuge in the stable, it was their own people who had crowded them out. It was the kinsmen of the Messiah who had no room for Him. Later, a divinely guided pen would write, "He came unto his own, and his own received him not." This rejection began at Bethlehem before His birth; it continued throughout His life and it followed His death.

Luke wasted no words in telling about the holy birth. He tersely stated, "And she brought forth her firstborn son, and wrapped him in swaddling clothes, and laid him in a manger." But in that sentence is stated the grandest of all truths—God had become flesh; the hopes of the centuries had been realized, for *Christ had come!* Christ in a baby blanket; Christ on a pile of straw; Christ in a manger; Christ in a stable!

Mary and Joseph could not give their Child the comforts and conveniences He deserved, but they gave Him a better gift—their love. The angels and the shepherds gave Him songs of praise, and the wise men gave Him gold, frankincense, and myrrh. But what Mary and Joseph gave Him was the best gift of all.

That is the gift He wants for Christmas—the gift of our love to Him. Like Mary and Joseph, we may wish we could do many things for Him. But what He wants most, each of us can give. Will you give Him your deepest love? That is what Christ wants for Christmas.

THINKING AND THANKING

To many persons, Thanksgiving is a season. To the Christian, thanksgiving should be a spirit.

The two worlds *think* and *thank* come from the same root word. One cannot think without having a basis for thanks. A brief pause to reflect on the goodness of God will quickly bring us to a spirit of thanksgiving.

As we think of what could have happened during the year and didn't, we are made to give thanks to God. When David was being pursued by jealous King Saul, he said to Jonathan, "There is but a step between me and death." (1 Sam. 20:3). Each of us could say the same for himself. Yet God has guided us safely through the year. As a poet said, the kind, restraining hand of Providence has overshadowed our lives.

Not only has God's protection been over our lives, He has also granted us a measure of health and wealth. For both, let us give thanks. How different things could have been! An unknown poet expressed this thought as follows:

The sun was shining in my eyes
And I could scarcely see
To do the necessary work
That was allotted me.
Resentful of the vivid glow,
I started to complain,
When all at once, upon the air,
I heard a blind man's cane.

In this age of affluence it is easy to take for granted the blessings that come to us. Worse yet is the danger of assuming that we have earned these material benefits by ourselves. We are warned in the Scriptures not to say, "The might of mine hand hath gotten me this wealth." (Deut. 8:17).

The Apostle Paul instructs us, "In every thing give thanks: for this is the will of God in Christ Jesus concerning you." (1 Thess. 5:18). Certainly this means that the life of the Christian is to be characterized by a spirit of thanksgiving. Topping the list of the many things for which we should be grateful is the gift of Christ Jesus himself. With Paul we say, "Thanks be unto God for his unspeakable gift." (2 Cor. 9:15).

Let us join with Principal Watt of New College, Edinburgh, who prayed, "Grant me one gift more-a grateful heart."

TIME

An old clock in a store in Linwood, Md., bears this inscription:

> *Lo! Here I stand by thee in plight,*
> *To give the warning day and night.*
> *For every tick to thee I give*
> *Cuts short the time thou hast to live.*

Time has an elusive quality about it. It cannot be bought, bartered, or borrowed; it can only be used. Time has no qualitative value in itself, its worth is calculated only in terms of how it is used.

In man's most desperate moments his driving desire is for more time. When a deadline is approaching and a task is not finished, one longs for more time. When facing death, one pleads for more time.

Time is unique in that it has no past and it has no future. Time is only in the present tense. When referring to time past, we speak of time that *was* once the present but is now forever gone. Time has no future; rather, it is metered out in moments of the present.

Ecclesiastes 3 tells us that there is a time to be born and a time to die. Between those two epochal events Solomon lists 26 examples of how time is to be used. All of those activities are present-oriented activities that must take place in the "now" that God grants.

In the summer of 1972, I watched scientists from Brigham Young University painstakingly remove the skeleton of a dinosaur from the dry, rocky soil of a mesa in western Colorado. It is called "supersaurus," the largest skeleton of a prehistoric animal found to date. Estimates of its age go back millions of years. That amount of time is mind-staggering. By comparison, it made me feel that my life is measured in seconds, not years. In reality, every life is measured in seconds. Rev. Charles Edwards stated the nature of time in the following lines:

> *Time was is past; thou canst not it recall;*
> *Time is thou hast; employ the portion small;*
> *Time future is not, and may never be;*
> *Time present is the only time for thee.*

Time must be used wisely. It is God's gift of the moment. There are no tomorrows; only todays, as God grants them.

On Arriving in Heaven

Within seconds of arriving there a voice behind me said, "I am in charge of your orientation." I turned and asked, "Who are you?"

He said, "Welcome, my name is Gabriel."

I said, "Gabriel, the archangel?"

He said, "Just call me Gabriel."

Then he asked, "Why did you get here?"

I said, "I was a minister for 65 years and not only that..." Gabriel put his hand on my shoulder and said, "Complete this Bible verse" – 'Not of works (I blushed and then murmured,) 'lest any man should boast." (Eph. 2:9).

Gabriel said, "Credentials are things of earth, not of heaven. Now finish the verse, 'For by grace are ye saved through faith and that not of yourselves...' Again, I mumbled, 'it is the gift of God."

Gabriel said, "All people here are God-gifted. You are here not by what you have earned, but by what you have been given."

Wanting to move from my embarrassment, I asked,

"Who is that man over there, the man wearing the strange hat, like the man on the box of oats?"

Gabriel said, "His name is George." Then it came to me, "He's George Fox, the great Quaker who began the Society of Friends in 1648."

"Yes," Gabriel said. "Just a short time ago."

"I told Gabriel that the Friends are good and godly people, quietly working in the world and making things better."

Gabriel said, "I know."

I was amazed at how intelligent Gabriel was.

Then I said, "Where is He? I want to see Him."

"You will see Him soon." Gabriel said.

Then Gabriel said, "How do you like it here?"

I said, "It's so wonderful, so unlike anything on earth." He said, "That is why it is called heaven."

I said, "It's so serene, so peaceful. I see smiles on all faces and it's so bright."

Gabriel said, "It's because of Him. He called himself the light of the world. He is also the light of the universe."

Gabriel asked, "What has surprised you most about heaven?"

I said, "There are no clocks and watches."

Gabriel said, "But we have time, plenty of it. It's called eternity."

I said, "On earth people are slaves to their watches. People do what their watches tell them to do – it's time to do this, it's time to do that and people obey. I pastored church that had a clock in the sanctuary. On its face were the words, 'It's time to seek the Lord,"

Gabriel said, "The time will come when there will be no time to seek the Lord."

I asked, "Who is that man over there?"

Gabriel said, "His name is Martin."

I said, "Who are the others who are talking with him?"

Gabriel said, "They are John, Charles and John C."

I said, "What does the C stand for?"

He replied, "We don't use last names here but I had to say John C. to distinguish him from the other man whose name is John. John C. is John Calvin."

Then it became clear to me. The men are Martin Luther, John and Charles Wesley and John Calvin, all of them fathers of denominations!

Gabriel said, "We do not use labels here."

I said, "Well, what do you call them?"

Gabriel said, "We call them Christians. They have been discussing theology for over 200 years and they have not fussed a single time."

I said, "Martin Luther was so busy teaching, preaching and writing that he had not changed bed lines for a year before he married Katharina von Bora. I didn't know that Lutherans did that! Katie must have turned her head, shaken the pillow out of its case, and held it at arm's length on her way outside to bury it."

I said, "Luther changed the course of history."

Gabriel said, "Yes, but remember that grace changed him before he changed history."

I pondered Gabriel's statement, "We do not use labels here." I asked him why that was so.

He said, "We don't go by what folks did, but by what they are."

I said, "Well what are they?"

Gabriel said, "Redeemed."

Then Gabriel said, "The Word asks a penetrating question: 'What hast thou that thou hast not received?' (1 Cor. 4:7). All who are in heaven gave much because they were given much."

I said, "I am yearning to see Him."

Gabriel replied, "You will see Him soon."

I looked up and said, "I know who that big man is — he's Peter the big fisherman who has a big mouth"

"Not now. It shrank on the day of Pentecost. Peter said more that day in one sermon than he had in the preceding 3 years. It was because he had been cleansed & empowered."

Gabriel said, "Do you see that beautiful woman over there? She's Teresa, Mother Teresa, as the world knew her. You should have heard her when she first arrived. She kept saying, "Where are they, where are they—the poor, the suffering and the dying—I must help them."

Gabriel said, "She went to sleep on earth and woke up here in heaven, not knowing her ministry was completed and I said, 'Teresa, you are in heaven where there are no tears, no death, sorrow, crying or pain.' (Rev. 21:4). She yanked off her hoodie thing, and shook out her beautiful blond hair, beamed, stood up strait and He wiped away her wrinkles.

She's a knockout!" I said to, "Gabriel!" and he blushed a bit.

I said, "What is all that clapping and shouting about?"

Gabriel said, "A soul has just been saved. As the Word says, there is joy in the presence of the angels of God over one sinner who repents. (Lk. 15:10) They are rejoicing. "We know about everything that goes on down there and it's all recorded in His books." I said, "Everything?" He said, "Everything."

I asked, "Who is that bright-eyed lady over there?" He said, "Her name is Fanny."

I said, "Blind Fanny Crosby? She wrote 8,000 hymns."

Gabriel said, "I hummed one today." Gabriel went on to say, "You should have seen her when she got here. She blinked a bit and then shrieked with joy and said, 'I see Him, I see Him!' We don't exaggerate here but, so help me, she leaped 15' and right into His open arms! His was the first face she ever saw!"

Then I recalled that she had written these words, "I shall see Him face to face and tell the story. "saved by grace." And another line, "I shall know my Redeemer when I reach the other side and his smile will be the first to welcome me."

Gabriel said, "Turn around." I turned and there He was! His arms were outstretched, not as they were when He was on the cross, but outstretched to me!

"I fell on my knees and cried holy, holy, holy. I clasped my hands and sang glory, glory to the Son of God." (Michael English)

Then I heard the voice of many angels and "The number of them was ten thousand times ten thousand, and thousands of thousands, saying with a loud voice, 'Worthy is the lamb that was slain to receive power and riches and wisdom and strength and honor and glory and blessing."
(Rev. 5:11, 12).

Benediction

"Now unto him that is able to keep you from falling, and to present you faultless before the presence of His glory with exceeding joy, to the only wise God our Saviour, be glory and majesty, dominion and power, both now and forever. Amen." (Jude 24, 25).